D1623910

THREE CLASSICS
IN THE AESTHETIC
OF MUSIC

Monsieur Croche the Dilettante Hater
by Claude Debussy

Sketch of a New Esthetic of Music
by Ferruccio Busoni

Essays before a Sonata
by Charles E. Ives

DOVER PUBLICATIONS, INC., NEW YORK

This new Dover edition, first published in 1962, is an unabridged and unaltered republication of the following:

Monsieur Croche the Dilettante Hater by Claude Debussy, as published by Noel Douglas in 1927. Translated by B. N. Langdon Davies. Copyright © 1928 by The Viking Press, Inc.

Sketch of a New Esthetic of Music by Ferruccio Busoni, as published by G. Schirmer, Inc., ca. 1911. Translated from the German by Dr. Th. Baker.

Essays before a Sonata by Charles E. Ives, as published by The Knickerbocker Press in 1920.

International Standard Book Number: 0-486-20320-4

Manufactured in the United States of America
Dover Publications, Inc.
180 Varick Street
New York, N.Y. 10014

Contents

Monsieur Croche the Dilettante Hater

Claude Debussy

Publisher's Note

The chapters of this book consist of articles which appeared in the *Revue Blanche* during 1901, *Gil Blas* during 1903-6, and in *Musica* during 1905 slightly altered, rearranged and added to by the author for publication in book form. The outbreak of war while the book was being printed caused it only to be issued in 1921 after Debussy's death. It appeared under the title *Monsieur Croche Antidilettante* in 1921, with the double imprint of the Librairie Dorbon Ainé and the *Nouvelle Revue Française*. In 1927 it was re-issued by the Librairie Gallimard, and it is from this edition that the present translation is made.

While the book is as a whole a brilliant and permanent contribution to musical criticism, it must not be forgotten that it was written as journalism, and that some of the allusions to current gossip and events are ephemeral and obscure. To this fact also are due one or two repetitions of phrases. The translators have tried to capture something of the subtle wit of the original. The individuality of the style, however, added to the fact that the author was not primarily a literary man and often allowed himself a certain freedom of construction and expression, has presented some difficulty and called at time for boldness in rendering his thought into the English language. Footnotes have been added where the information seemed necessary or interesting.

Léon Vallas' book, *Les Idées de Claude Debussy*, of which an English translation by Maire O'Brien will be issued by the Oxford University Press in 1928, is a clear and simple co-ordination of Debussy's musical views based on his articles, of which the most important were selected by him for the present book.

I Monsieur Croche the Dilettante Hater

It was a lovely evening. I had decided to idle. I mean, of course, that I was dreaming. I do not want to imply that anything of great emotional value was happening or that I was laying the foundations of the Future. I was just enjoying that occasional care-free mood which brings peace with all the world.

And of what was I dreaming? What were my limits? What was the goal of my work? Questions, I fear, prompted by a somewhat childish egotism and the craving to escape from an ideal with which one has lived too long! Questions, moreover, that are but a thin disguise for the foolish yearning to be regarded as superior to others! The struggle to surpass others has never been really great if dissociated from the noble ideal of surpassing oneself—though this, involving as it does the sacrifice of one's cherished personality, implies a very special kind of alchemy. Besides, superiority over others is difficult to maintain and gives in the end but a barren victory. The pursuit of universal approbation means the waste of a great deal of time in continual demonstration and sedulous self-advertisement. These things may win one the honour of inclusion in a collection of distinguished persons whose names are used as the sauce for insipid conversations on art. But I will not labour the point. I should not like to check ambition.

The evening was as lovely as ever, but, as must already be obvious, I was out of humour with myself—I had lost grip and found that I was drifting into the most irritating generalisations.

At this precise moment my door-bell rang and I made the acquaintance of Monsieur Croche. It is unnecessary to check the flow of this narrative with the obvious or trifling incidents of his first visit.

Monsieur Croche was a spare, wizened man and his gestures were obviously suited to the conduct of metaphysical discussions; his features are best pictured by recalling those of Tom Lane, the jockey, and M. Thiers. He spoke almost in a whisper and never laughed, occasionally enforcing his remarks with a quiet smile which, beginning at his nose, wrinkled his whole face, like a pebble flung into still waters, and lasted for an intolerably long time.

He aroused my curiosity at once by his peculiar views on music. He spoke of an orchestral score as if it were a picture. He seldom used technical words, but the dimmed and slightly worn elegance of his rather unusual vocabulary seemed to ring like old coins. I remember a parallel he drew between Beethoven's orchestration—which he visualised as a black-and-white formula resulting in an exquisite gradation of greys—and that of Wagner, a sort of many-coloured "make-up" spread almost uniformly, in which, he said, he could no longer distinguish the tone of a violin from that of a trombone.

Since his intolerable smile was especially evident when he talked of music, I suddenly decided to ask him what his profession might be. He replied in a voice which checked any attempt at comment: "Dilettante Hater." Then he went on monotonously and irritably:

"Have you noticed the hostility of a concert-room audience? Have you studied their almost drugged expression of boredom, indifference and even stupidity? They never grasp the noble dramas woven into the symphonic conflict in which one is conscious of the possibility of reaching the summit of the structure of harmony and breathing there an atmosphere of perfect beauty. Such people always seem like guests who are more or less well-bred; they endure the tedium of their position with patience, and they remain only because they wish to be seen taking their leave at the end; otherwise, why come? You must admit that this is a good reason for an eternal hatred of music."

I argued that I had observed and had even shared in highly commendable displays of enthusiasm. To which he answered:

"You are greatly in error; for, if you showed so much enthusiasm, it was with the secret hope that some day a similar honour would be paid to you. Surely you know that a genuine appreciation of beauty can only result in silence? Tell me, when you see the daily wonder of the sunset have you ever thought of applauding? Yet you will admit that it is a rather more unrehearsed effect than all your musical trifles. More-over, face to face with the sunset you feel so mean a thing that you cannot become a part of it. But before a so-called work of art you are yourself and you have a classical jargon which gives you an opportunity for eloquence."

I dared not confess how nearly I agreed with him, since nothing withers conversation like agreement. I preferred to ask if he himself played any instrument. He raised his head sharply and replied:

"I dislike specialists. Specialisation is for me the narrow-ing of my universe. It reminds me of those old horses who, in bygone days, worked the roundabouts and died to the well-known strains of the *Marche Lorraine!*[1] Nevertheless, I know all music and it has only given me a special pride in being safe from every kind of surprise. Two bars suffice to give me the clue to a symphony, or to any other musical incident.

"Though we may be certain that some great men have a stubborn determination always to break fresh ground, it is not so with many others, who do nothing but repeat the thing in which they have once succeeded. Their skill leaves me cold. They have been hailed as Masters. Beware lest this be not a polite method of getting rid of them or of excusing the sameness of their performances. In short, I try to forget music because it obscures my perception of what I do not know or shall only know to-morrow. Why cling to something one knows too well?"

I mentioned the most famous of our contemporaries and Monsieur Croche was more aggressive than ever.

"I am much more interested in sincere and honestly felt impressions than in criticism, which often enough resembles brilliant variations on the theme: 'Since you do not agree with me, you are mistaken'; or else: 'You have talent, I have none; it is useless to go any further.' In all compositions I endeavour to fathom the diverse impulses inspiring them and their inner life. Is not this much more interesting than the game of pulling them to pieces, like curious watches?

"People forget that, as children, they were forbidden to pull their jumping-jacks to pieces—even then such behaviour was

[1] Orchestral military march by Louis Ganne.

treason against the mysteries—and they continue to want to poke their aesthetic noses where they have no business to be. Though they no longer rip open puppets, yet they explain, pull to pieces and in cold blood slay the mysteries; it is comparatively easy; moreover you can chat about it. Well, well! an obvious lack of understanding excuses some of them; but others, act with greater ferocity and premeditation, for they must of necessity protect their cherished little talents. These last have a loyal following.

"I am only slightly concerned with works hallowed either by success or tradition: once and for all, Meyerbeer,[1] Thalberg,[2] and Reyer,[3] are men of genius; otherwise they are of no importance.

"On Sundays, when God is kind, I hear no music: please accept my apologies. Finally, be so good as to note the word 'impressions' which is applicable, since it leaves me free to preserve my emotion from all superfluous aestheticism.

"You are inclined to exaggerate events which, in Bach's day, would have appeared natural. You talk to me about Dukas'[4] sonata. He is probably one of your friends and even a musical critic. Good reasons for speaking well of him. Your praise, however, has been surpassed; for Pierre Lalo,[5] in an article in *Le Temps,* devoted exclusively to this sonata, made simultaneous sacrifice to Dukas of the sonatas written by Schumann and Chopin. As a matter of fact, Chopin's nervous temperament was ill-adapted to the endurance needed for the construction of a sonata: he made elaborate 'first drafts.' Yet we may say that Chopin inaugurated a special method of treating this form, not to mention the charming artistry which he devised in this connection. He was fertile in ideas, which he often invested without demanding that hundred per cent. on

---

[1] Giacomo Meyerbeer, born Berlin, 1791; died, Paris, 1864; composed the highly successful operas, *Robert le Diable, Les Huguenots, Le Prophète, etc.*

[2] Sigismund Thalberg, born Geneva, 1812; died, 1871. Although this composer and artist had a great vogue in his time and exercised some influence on other composers, his works are now practically forgotten.

[3] Ernest Louis Etienne Rey, born Marseilles, 1823, died, 1909; known under the name of Reyer, which he considered more suitable to a musical career, as the composer of the operas, *Sigurd, Salammbo,* etc.

[4] Paul Dukas, born Paris, 1865; the composer of *Ariane et Barbebleue,* etc.

[5] Pierre Lalo, born 1866; composer and musical critic of *Le Temps.*

the transaction which is the brightest halo of some of our Masters.

"Lalo, of course, evokes the noble shade of Beethoven in reference to the sonata of your friend Dukas. Personally, I should have been only mildly flattered! Beethoven's sonatas are very badly written for the piano; they are, particularly those that came later, more accurately described as orchestral transcriptions. There seems often to be lacking a third hand which I am sure Beethoven heard; at least I hope so. It would have been safer to leave Schumann and Chopin alone; undoubtedly they wrote for the piano; and if that is not enough for Lalo, he ought at least to be grateful to them for having opened a way towards the perfection represented by a Dukas—and incidentally some others."

Monsieur Croche uttered these last words with an imperturbable detachment: a challenge to be taken up or ignored. I was too much interested to take it up and left him to continue. There was a long silence, during which there came from him no sign of life save for the smoke ascending in blue spirals from his cigar which he watched curiously as if he were contemplating strange distortions—perhaps bold systems. His silence became disconcerting and rather alarming. At length he resumed:

"Music is a sum total of scattered forces. You make an abstract ballad of them! I prefer the simple notes of an Egyptian shepherd's pipe; for he collaborates with the landscape and hears harmonies unknown to your treatises. Musicians listen only to the music written by cunning hands, never to that which is in nature's script. To see the sun rise is more profitable than to hear the *Pastoral Symphony*. What is the use of your almost incomprehensible art? Ought you not to suppress all the parasitical complexities which make music as ingenious as the lock of a strong-box? You paw the ground because you only know music and submit to strange and barbarous laws. You are hailed with high-sounding praises, but you are merely cunning! Something between a monkey and a lackey."

I ventured to say that some had tried in poetry, others in painting—I added with some trepidation one or two musicians—to shake off the ancient dust of tradition and it had only resulted in their being treated as symbolists or impressionists —convenient terms for pouring scorn on one's fellows.

"It is only journalists and hucksters who treat them so," Monsieur Croche continued without a falter, "and it is of no importance. A beautiful idea in embryo has in it something absurd for fools. There is a surer hope of beauty in such derided men than in those poor sheep who flock docilely to the slaughter-houses which a discerning fate has prepared for them.

"To be unique, faultless! The enthusiasm of society spoils an artist for me, such is my fear that, as a result, he will become merely an expression of society.

"Discipline must be sought in freedom, and not within the formulas of an outworn philosophy only fit for the feeble-minded. Give ear to no man's counsel; but listen to the wind which tells in passing the history of the world."

As he spoke Monsieur Croche appeared to be lit up from within. I seemed to see into him and his words came to me like some strange music. I cannot adequately convey his peculiar eloquence. Something like this, perhaps:

"Do you know anything more splendid than to discover by chance a genius who has been unrecognized through the ages? But to have been such a genius oneself—can any glory equal it?"

Day was breaking; Monsieur Croche was visibly fatigued and went away. I accompanied him as far as the landing door; he no more thought of shaking my hand than I of thanking him. For a considerable time I listened to the sound of his steps dying away flight by flight. I dared not hope that I should ever see him again.

II   A Talk about the Prix de Rome and Saint-Saëns

Irresistibly bewitched by the magic of the ancient forests I had stayed late one autumn day in the country. From the fall of the golden leaves that invest the splendid obsequies of the trees, from the clear angelus that calls the fields to rest, rose a gentle and alluring voice counselling oblivion. The sun was setting in its solitude; no peasants were inspired to take lithographic poses in the foreground. Beasts and men were returning peacefully, having completed some common task whose beauty had this special distinction, that it called no more for encouragement than for disapprobation. Remote were those discussions on art in which the very names of great men sometimes seemed to be words of abuse. Forgotten was the petty artificial feverishness of the "first-night." I was alone, pleasantly care-free; perhaps I had never loved music more than at this moment when I heard no talk of it. It apeared to me in its complete beauty, not in the hectic scantiness of trivial symphonic or lyrical fragments. Now and again I thought of Monsieur Croche; for he has an unobtrusive and shadowy personality which can be fitted into any landscape without interfering with its composition. But I had to leave these calm joys and to return, impelled by that superstition of the town which makes many men prefer to be hustled sooner than not to be a part of the movement of which they are the creaking and unconscious works. As I was passing along the fashionable sameness of the Boulevard Malesherbes in the drab twilight, I caught sight of the spare figure of Monsieur Croche and, taking advantage of his eccentric habits, I fell into step beside him without further ceremony. A quick glance assured me of his acquiescence and presently he began to speak in his quaint asthmatic voice, intensified now by the rawness of the air which gave a strange quality of tone to every word he uttered.

"Among the institutions on which France prides herself, do you know any more ridiculous than the institution of the *Prix de Rome*?[1] I am aware that this has often been said and still more often written, but apparently without any effect, since

1 L'Ecole nationale et spéciale des beaux-arts, under the direction of the Bureau de l'enseignement, gives instruction in the arts and holds competitions, among which is that for the *Prix de Rome*. The final award is made by the judges in all sections of the Institute (L'Académie des beaux-arts) acting together. This award entitles the holder to a period of free travel and residence at the Académie de France in the Villa Medicis at Rome. The foundation of the Académie in 1666 has been variously attributed to Poussin, Le Brun, or Charles Errard. It was for pupils capable of profiting thereby to continue their studies in Italy. The competition for the *Prix de Rome* was established by decree in 1871.

it continues to exist with that deplorable obstinacy which distinguishes absurd ideas."

I ventured to answer that possibly the institution derived its strength from the fact that it had attained in certain circles to the position of a superstition. To have won or not to have won the *Prix de Rome* settled the question of whether one did or did not possess talent. If it was not absolutely certain, it was at least convenient and provided public opinion with a sort of ready-reckoner.

Monsieur Croche whistled through his teeth—to himself, I suppose.

"Yes, you won the *Prix de Rome*—Observe, sir, that I readily admit that one should help young people to travel peacefully in Italy and even in Germany; but why restrict them to those two countries? Above all, why the vexatious diploma which puts them on a plane with fat cattle?

"The *Prix de Rome* is a game; or, rather, a national sport. The rules are taught in places called Conservatoires, Art Schools, etc.

"The contests, preceded by strict training, take place once a year and the umpires of the game are members of the Institute; hence the curious fact that Bouguereau[1] and Massenet[2] judge these games indifferently whether played in music, painting, sculpture, architecture or engraving. No one has yet thought of including a dancer amongst them, though that would be logical, Terpsichore being not the most negligible of the nine Muses.

"Without wishing to discredit the institution of the *Prix de Rome,* we may at least maintain its lack of foresight. By that I mean to suggest that very young people are cynically given over to the fascinating temptations of a boundless liberty; a liberty, moreover, which they do not know how to use. They have to fulfil the conditions in the book of rules which controls the movements of 'travelling students,' and lo! they are relieved of any further responsibility. When they arrive in Rome, how-

[1] The French painter, William Bouguereau, born and died at La Rochelle, 1825-1905.

[2] Jules Massenet, the composer of the operas *Le Cid, Manon, Thaïs, La Navarraise, Werther,* etc.; born Saint-Etienne, 1842; died Paris, 1912.

ever, the limited knowledge they possess is of their own craft alone! These young people, confused at the outset by an utter change in their way of life, are expected to provide for themselves the inspirational energy needful to the soul of an artist. This is impossible! And anyone who reads the annual report on the travelling students will be amazed at the severity of its terms; nor are the holders of studentships to blame if their canons are somewhat confused; one should rather blame those who send them to a country redolent everywhere of the purest art, whilst leaving them free to interpret that art in their own way. Further, is not the academic detachment of the gentlemen of the Institute, who decide which among a number of young persons shall be an artist, astonishing in its ingenuousness? What do they know about it? Are they so sure of being artists themselves? On what then do they base their claim to control so enigmatical a destiny? Would it not, indeed, be better for them to have recourse to the simple method of drawing lots? Who knows? Chance is sometimes so inspired! No, we must look elsewhere—Never judge by works on set themes, or of such a character that it is impossible to know for certain whether the young people know their business as musicians. Let them receive a certificate for a high level of attainment, if that is what is wanted; but no certificate for imagination, since that is useless and grotesque! Once this formality is fulfilled, let them travel across Europe; let them choose a recognised master for themselves; or, if they can find him, a sensible fellow who can teach them that art is not necessarily restricted to works subsidised by the State!"

Monsieur Croche paused to cough distressingly, for which he blamed his cigar, which had gone out.

"We argue," said he, holding it up, "and this goes out, ironically accusing me of talking too much, warning me that finally it will bury me under a heap of ash: an attractively pantheistic funeral pyre, you will admit, and a mild comment on the fact that one should not believe oneself indispensable, and that one should accept the brevity of life as the most useful of precepts."

Then he turned abruptly to me:

"On Sunday I was at *Lamoureux's*,[1] where they hissed your music. You ought to be grateful to an audience for being sufficiently moved to take the trouble to blow down keys—implements usually considered with justice to be domestic, and therefore unsuitable as weapons of warfare. The method of butcher-boys whistling through their fingers is much to be preferred. One lives and learns. Chevillard, on this occasion, showed once again an astounding and manifold knowledge of music. As to the *Choral Symphony*,[2] his vigour and decision in performance are such that he seems to be playing it by himself; he more than merited the praises usually showered on him."

I could only acquiesce, merely adding that since I did my best to write music for its own sake and disinterestedly, it was logical that I should run the risk of displeasing people who are so devoted to one musical method that they remain faithfully blind to its wrinkles or cosmetics.

"The people of whom we speak," he went on, "are not to blame. You ought, rather, to blame the artists who perform the barren task of ministering to and maintaining the deliberate indifference of the public. In addition to this offence, these same artists know how to strive just long enough to gain a footing in the market-place; but, the sale of their goods once assured, they retire promptly, seeming to apologise to the public for the trouble it has taken to admit them. They wallow in success, resolutely turning their backs on their youth. They are never able to rise to a fame happily reserved for men whose lives, consecrated to the search for a world of ever-renewed sensations and forms, have ended in the joyous conviction of a noble task accomplished. Such men have obtained what may be termed a 'last night' success—if success be not too mean a word for what is glory.

"Finally, to take a recent example, I am sorry to see how difficult it is to keep one's respect for an artist who was once filled with enthusiasm and a thirst for pure glory. I hate senti-

1 Charles Lamoureux, the founder of the celebrated Paris concerts bearing his name, born Bordeaux, 1834; died Paris, 1899. His son-in-law, Camille Chevillard, became his assistant and continued the concerts after Lamoureux's death.

2 Beethoven's 9th Symphony in D minor, op. 125.

mentality! But I wish I could forget that his name is Camille Saint-Saëns!"[1]

I merely answered:

"I have listened to *Les Barbares.*"

He continued with an emotion I had not expected from him:

"How is it possible to go so completely wrong? Saint-Saëns knows the world's music better than anyone. How could he forget that he made known and compelled recognition for the turbulent genius of Liszt? How could he forget his worship of the elder Bach?

"Why this itch to write operas and to descend from Louis Gallet[2] to Victorien Sardou,[3] spreading the detestable error that it is necessary to 'write for the stage?' A thing never compatible with 'writing music.' "

I offered a few timid objections, such as:

"Is *Les Barbares* worse than many other operas mentioned by you? Should it make us forget the earlier Saint-Saëns?"

Monsieur Croche interrupted sharply:

"That opera is worse than the others just because it is by Saint-Saëns. He owed it to himself, and still more to music, never to have written that romance embodying a little of everything, even a farandole, of which they praise the 'archaic savour'; it is a feeble echo of that 'Street in Cairo' that was the success of the 1889 Exhibition; its archaism is dubious. Running all through it is a painful seeking for effect, suggested by a libretto containing tags for the suburbs and situations which, by their very nature, make the music absurd. The mimicry of the singers and the traditional sardine-box staging, so grimly preserved by the Opera, polishes off the performance and any hope of art.

"Does no one care sufficiently for Saint-Saëns to tell him

---

1 Charles Camille Saint-Saëns, the composer of the operas *Samson et Dalila* and *Les Barbares, La Danse Macabre,* etc., born Paris, 1835.

2 Louis Gallet, born Valence, Drôme, 1835; died 1898; was a well-known writer of libretti. Among his best-known works are *Le Cid, Thaïs, L'Attaque du Moulin,* etc.

3 The French dramatic writer, Victorien Sardou, born Paris, 1831; died 1908. Among his best-known works are *Madame Sans-Gêne, La Tosca, Les Pattes-de-Mouche.*

he has written music enough and that he would be better employed in following his belated vocation of explorer?"[1]

Monsieur Croche was tempted by another cigar and said to me by way of farewell:

"Forgive me, but I should not like to spoil this one."

Since I had gone far past my home, I retraced my steps, thinking of Monsieur Croche and of his morose impartiality. Looking at it broadly, it showed a little of the resentment we feel for those whom we have once deeply loved and whose slightest change seems treachery. I tried, too, to picture Saint-Saëns on the evening of the first performance of *Les Barbares* recalling, amid the applause which greeted his name, the sound of the hisses which welcomed the first hearing of his *Danse Macabre*,[2] and I liked to think that such a memory was not distasteful to him.

Then I thought of years now far distant.

My happiest impressions connected with the *Prix de Rome* were independent of it. I was on the Pont des Arts awaiting the result of the competition and watching with delight the scurrying of the little Seine steamers. I was quite calm, having forgotten all emotion due to anything Roman, so seductive was the charm of the gay sunshine playing on the ripples, a charm which keeps those delightful idlers, who are the envy of Europe, hour after hour on the bridges.

Suddenly somebody tapped me on the shoulder, and said breathlessly:

"You've won the prize!"

Believe me or not, I can assure you that all my pleasure vanished! I saw in a flash the boredom, the vexations inevitably incident to the slightest official recognition. Besides, I felt that I was no longer free.

These impressions soon faded: we cannot immediately be insensible of that little ray of provisional glory which the *Prix de Rome* gives: and when I reached the Villa Medicis,[3] in 1885, I almost thought I must be that darling of the gods told of in ancient legends.

[1] This, no doubt, refers to Saint-Saëns' extended musical tours in Europe and even in northern Africa.

[2] See Note 1, p. 13.

[3] See Note p. 9.

Cabat,[1] a reputable landscape painter as well as a man of the world of some distinction, was Director of the Académie de France[2] in Rome at the time. He never interfered with the students, save in an administrative capacity. He was delightful. Hébert[3] succeeded him soon after. I gathered from a recent conversation that this eminent painter has remained "Roman" to the very finger-tips. Indeed his intolerance of anything against Rome and the Villa Medicis is proverbial. He would allow no criticism on those two subjects; and I still remember how, when I complained of being housed in a room with walls painted green, which seemed to me to retreat as I approached them —a room well known to students as the "Etruscan Tomb"— Hébert assured me that it was of no importance. He even added that one could, if necessary, sleep among the ruins of the Coliseum. The blessing of experiencing a "historic tremor" would compensate for the risk of catching fever.

Hébert loved music passionately, but Wagner's music not at all. At that time I was a Wagnerian to the pitch of forgetting the simplest rules of courtesy, nor did I imagine that I could ever come almost to agree with this enthusiastic old man who had travelled through all these emotions with his eyes open, whereas we hardly grasped their meaning or how to use them.

Then began that student life, which has something in common with the life of a cosmopolitan hotel, a free college, and the discipline of a hostel. I can recall the dining-room at the Villa, lined with portraits of *Prix de Rome* winners, ancient and modern. They reached to the ceiling, becoming almost indiscernible; it is quite true that no one ever talks about them now. Each face wears the same rather dejected expression; they seem out of their element. After a lapse of several months the multiplicity of these frames with their fixed dimensions makes the beholder feel that the same prize-winner is repeated to infinity!

The conversations at the table very much resemble the

1 The French landscape painter, Louis Nicolas Cabat, born and died Paris, 1812-1893, was one of the founders of the modern school of landscape painting.

2 See Note p. 9.

3 Ernest Hébert, French painter of historical subjects and portraits, born and died Grenoble, 1817-1908.

gossip at a *table d'hôte*, and it would be idle to imagine that new theories of art, or even the burning dreams of the old masters are discussed. Though the Villa Medicis is therefore a mediocre home of Art, it is nevertheless a very rapid school for the practical side of life, so large looms the thought of the figure one will cut on one's return to Paris. Intercourse with Roman society is virtually non-existent, since its inaccessibility equals its self-sufficiency, and the youthful and thoroughly French independence of a student's mind consorts ill with Roman frigidity. Travel through Italy remains the only resource: a poor resource, from which it is impossible to derive the desired profit owing to a lack of connections in the towns through which one passes as a foreigner. Such connections could be easily established, since a little thought would provide the remedy. The best one can do is to buy photographs, the patience of the young women engaged in that trade being as unlimited as their smiles.

I was never again to meet Monsieur Croche. But do not the ghosts of hushed voices wait on us all? It is only just, therefore, to attribute to him a large share in the following pages, although I realise my inability to differentiate clearly between the speakers in an imaginary conversation.

III   *The Symphony*

A fog of verbiage and criticism surrounds the *Choral Symphony*.[1] It is amazing that it has not been finally buried under the mass of prose which it has provoked. Wagner intended to complete the orchestration. Others fancied that they could explain and illustrate the theme by means of pictures. If we admit to a mystery in this Symphony we might clear it up; but is it worth while? There was not an ounce of literature in Beethoven, not at any rate in the accepted sense of the word. He had a great love of music, representing

---

1 Beethoven's 9th Symphony in D minor, op. 125. The last movement is nominally a setting of Schiller's *Hymn to Joy*, with full orchestra, full choir and four solo singers.

to him, as it did, the joy and passion piteously absent from his private life. Perhaps we ought in the *Choral Symphony* to look for nothing more than a magnificent gesture of musical pride. A little notebook with over two hundred different renderings of the dominant theme in the *Finale* of this Symphony shows how persistently Beethoven pursued his search and how entirely musical his guiding motive was; Schiller's lines can have only been used for their appeal to the ear. Beethoven determined that his leading idea should be essentially self-developing and, while it is of extraordinary beauty in itself, it becomes sublime because of its perfect response to his purpose. It is the most triumphant example of the moulding of an idea to the pre-conceived form; at each leap forward there is a new delight, without either effort or appearance of repetition; the magical blossoming, so to speak, of a tree whose leaves burst forth simultaneously. Nothing is superfluous in this stupendous work, not even the *Andante,* declared by modern æstheticism to be over long; is it not a subtly conceived pause between the persistent rhythm of the *Scherzo* and the instrumental flood that rolls the voices irresistibly onward to the glory of the *Finale?* Beethoven had already written eight symphonies and the figure nine seems to have had for him an almost mystic significance. He determined to surpass himself. I can scarcely see how his success can be questioned. The flood of human feeling which overflows the ordinary bounds of the symphony sprang from a soul drunk with liberty, which, by an ironical decree of fate, beat itself against the gilded bars within which the misdirected charity of the great had confined him. Beethoven must have suffered cruelly in his ardent longing that humanity should find utterance through him; hence the call of his thousand-voiced genius to the humblest and poorest of his brethren. Did they hear it? That is the question. Recently the *Choral Symphony* was performed together with several of Richard Wagner's highly-spiced masterpieces. Once again Tannhäuser, Siegmund and Lohengrin voiced the claims of the *leit-motif!* The stern and loyal mastery of our great Beethoven easily triumphed over this vague and high-flown charlatanism.

It seems to me that the proof of the futility of the symphony has been established since Beethoven. Indeed, Schumann and Mendelssohn did no more than respectfully repeat the same forms with less power. The Ninth Symphony none the less was a demonstration of genius, a sublime desire to augment and to liberate the usual forms by giving them the harmonious proportions of a fresco.

Beethoven's real teaching then was not to preserve the old forms, still less to follow in his early steps. We must throw wide the windows to the open sky; they seem to me to have only just escaped being closed for ever. The fact that here and there a genius succeeds in this form is but a poor excuse for the laborious and stilted compositions which we are accustomed to call symphonies.

The young Russian school has endeavoured to give new life to the symphony by borrowing ideas from popular melodies; it has succeeded in cutting brilliant gems; but are not the themes entirely disproportionate to the developments into which they have been forced? Yet the fashion for popular airs has spread quickly throughout the musical world—from east to west the tiniest villages have been ransacked and simple tunes, plucked from the mouths of hoary peasants, find themselves, to their consternation, trimmed with harmonic frills. This gives them an appearance of pathetic discomfort, but a lordly counterpoint ordains that they shall forget their peaceful origin.

Must we conclude that the symphony, in spite of so many attempted transformations, belongs to the past by virtue of its studied elegance, its formal elaboration and the philosophical and artificial attitude of its audience? Has it not in truth merely replaced its old tarnished frame of gold with the stubborn brass of modern instrumentation?

A symphony is usually built up on a chant heard by the composer as a child. The first section is the customary presentation of a theme on which the composer proposes to work; then begins the necessary dismemberment; the second section seems to take place in an experimental laboratory; the third section cheers up a little in a quite childish way interspersed with deeply sentimental phrases during which the chant withdraws as is more seemly; but it reappears and the dismemberment goes on; the professional gentlemen, obviously interested, mop their brows and the audience calls for the composer. But the composer does not appear. He is engaged in listening modestly to the voice of tradition which prevents him, it seems to me, from hearing the voice that speaks within him.

IV   *Moussorgski*

Moussorgski's *Nursery* is a suite of seven melodies, each a scene from childhood. It is a masterpiece. Moussorgski is not well-known in France; for which we may be excused by pointing out that he is no better known in Russia. He was born at Karevo, Central Russia, in 1839 and he died in 1881 in the Nicholas Military Hospital, St. Petersburg.

It is evident that he had not very long for the development of his genius; and he lost no time, for he will leave an indelible impression on the minds of those who love him or will love him in the future. No one has given utterance to the best within us in tones more gentle or profound: he is unique, and will remain so, because his art is spontaneous and free from arid formulas. Never has a more refined sensibility been conveyed by such simple means; it is like the art of an enquiring savage discovering music step by step through his emotions. Nor is there ever a question of any particular form; at all events the form is so varied that by no possibility whatsoever can it be related to any established, one might say official, form, since it depends on and is made up of successive minute touches mysteriously linked together by means of an instinctive clairvoyance.

Sometimes, too, Moussorgski conveys shadowy sensations of trembling anxiety which move and wring the heart. In the *Nursery* there is the prayer of a little girl before she falls asleep which conveys the thoughts and the sensitive emotions of a child, the delightful ways of little girls pretending to be grown-up; all with a sort of feverish truth of interpretation only to be found here. The *Doll's Lullaby* would seem to have been conceived word by word, through an amazing power of sympathetic interpretation and of visualizing the realms of that special fairyland peculiar to the mind of a child. The end of the lullaby is so gently drowsy that the little singer falls asleep over her own fancies. Here too is the dreadful little boy astride a stick turning the room into a battlefield, now smashing the arms and now the legs of the poor defenceless chairs. He cannot do this without hurting himself too. Then we hear tears and screams; happiness vanishes. It is nothing serious; a moment on his mother's lap, a healing kiss, and the battle starts afresh and again the chairs do not know where to hide.

All these little dramas are set down, I repeat, with the utmost simplicity; Moussorgski was content with a construction which would have seemed paltry to Mr.——I forget his name! or with so instinctive a modulation that it would be quite beyond the range of Mr.—— the same fellow! We shall have more to say about Moussorgski; he has many claims to our devotion.

V   *The Paul Dukas Sonata*

Music, nowadays, tends to become more and more an accompaniment for sentimental or tragic incidents, and plays the ambiguous part of the showman at the door of a booth behind which is displayed the sinister form of "Mr. Nobody."

True lovers of music seldom frequent fairs; they merely have a piano and feverishly play a few pages over and over again; as sure a means of intoxication as "just, subtle and mighty opium," and the least enervating way of spending happy hours. Paul Dukas[1] seems to have had such people in mind when writing his sonata. It breathes a kind of mystic emotion and presents a rigidly connected sequence of ideas which seem to compel a close and careful study. This compelling quality gives a peculiar stamp to nearly all the work of Paul Dukas, even when it is merely episodic. It is the result of the patient intensity with which he adjusts the several parts of his harmonic scheme. It is to be feared that such work may prove difficult to follow on a concert platform. No reflection is thereby cast on either the beauty or the vision of the sonata. Although the mind conceiving this work unites a constructive purpose with an imagina-

1 See Note 4, p. 6.

tive idea, there is no need to assume a desire for complexity; nothing could be more deliberately absurd.

Paul Dukas knows the potentialities of music; it is not merely a matter of brilliant tone playing upon the listener to the point of enervation, an easy thing to understand where several kinds of music which seem antagonistic are united without difficulty. For him music is an inexhaustible store of forms, of pregnant memories which allow him to mould his ideas to the limits of his imaginative world. He is the master of his emotion and knows how to keep it from noisy futility. That is why he never indulges in those parasitic developments which so often disfigure the most beautiful effects. When we consider the third movement of his sonata, we discover under the picturesque surface an energy that guides the rhythmic fantasy with the silent precision of steel mechanism. The same energy prevails in the last part, where the art of distributing emotion appears in its highest form; one might even call this emotion constructive, since it displays a beauty akin to perfect lines in architecture, lines that dissolve into and are keyed to the spatial colour of air and sky, the whole being wedded in a complete and final harmony.

VI Virtuosos

During the last few weeks there has been a great influx of German conductors. This is not as serious as an epidemic, though it makes more noise, a conductor being multiplied by ninety. I do not deny that Weingartner[1] or Richard Strauss,[2] Mottl[3] with his vigour or the great Richter,[4] may make the outraged beauty of the Masters blossom anew, but there is

1 The celebrated conductor and composer, Paul Felix Weingartner, was born Zara, Dalmatia, in 1863.

2 Richard Strauss, the famous conductor and composer of *Salome, Elektra, Der Rosenkavalier,* etc., was born Munich, 1864.

3 Felix Mottl, the well-known conductor, born Unter St. Veit, near Vienna, 1856; died 1911; conducted the Vienna Wagner Society, and in 1876 assisted in staging *The Ring* at Bayreuth.

4 See Note 2, p. 59.

no necessity to go too far, as if Paris were a training school. If only these gentlemen would introduce some novelty into their programmes it might be interesting, but they do not. They offer the same old symphonic stock-in-trade and we shall have the usual demonstrations of the different methods of conducting Beethoven's symphonies. Some of them hurry the symphonies, others drag them; and the greatest sufferer will be poor old Beethoven. Pompous well-informed persons will declare that such and such a conductor has the secret of the true tempo; anyhow, it makes an excellent subject of conversation. How do these people come to be so sure? Have they received word from the Beyond? That would be a courtesy from the other world which would surprise me very much in Beethoven. If his unhappy spirit occasionally wanders into a concert room, surely it returns hurriedly to the realms where only the music of the spheres is heard! His noble ancestor, Bach, must say to him with some severity:

"My little Ludwig, I see by your somewhat rumpled soul that you have again been in disreputable places."

But perhaps they are not on speaking terms.

The attraction of the virtuoso for the public is very like that of the circus for the crowd. There is always a hope that something dangerous may happen: Mr. X may play the violin with Mr. Y on his shoulders; or Mr. Z may conclude his piece by lifting the piano with his teeth.[1]

X plays Bach's violin concerto in G, as perhaps he alone can without seeming to be an interloper; for he has that freedom of expression, that unaffected beauty of tone, which are essential for its interpretation.

This is all the more noticeable since the rest of the performance moves painfully and heavily. It might be said that this rigid method of interpretation compels the works of Bach to carry the weight of all the ages.

Yet the beauty of this concerto stands out from among the others which appear in Bach's manuscripts; it contains, almost intact, that musical arabesque, or rather that principle of

---

[1] The original article read: "M. Ysaye may play the violin with M. Colonne on his shoulders; or M. Pugno may conclude his piece by lifting the piano with his teeth."

ornament, which is the basis of all forms of art. The word "ornament" has here nothing whatever to do with the meaning attached to it in the musical grammars.

The primitives, Palestrina,[1] Vittoria,[2] Orlando di Lasso[3] and others, made use of this divine arabesque. They discovered the principle in the Gregorian chant; and they strengthened the delicate traceries by strong counterpoint. When Bach went back to the arabesque he made it more pliant and more fluid; and, in spite of the stern discipline which the great composer imposed on beauty, there was a freshness and freedom in his imaginative development of it which astonishes us to this day.

In Bach's music it is not the character of the melody that stirs us, but rather the tracing of a particular line, often indeed of several lines, whose meeting, whether by chance or design, makes the appeal. Through this conception of ornament the music acquires an almost mechanical precision of appeal to which the audience reacts.

Let no one think that there is anything unnatural or artificial in this. It is infinitely more "true" than the wretched whimperings and the tentative wailings of lyric drama. Above all, the music keeps all its dignity; it never lowers itself by truckling to the desire for sentimentality of those of whom it is said that "they do so love music"; with greater pride it compels their respect, if not their worship.

It is most noticeable that no one was ever known to whistle Bach. Such lip service has not been denied to Wagner when the doors of the concert rooms are opened and the pampered prisoners are released from their padded seats and there is heard in the streets the cheerful whistling of the *Spring Song*[4] or of the opening phrase of the *Meistersingers*. I am well aware that, for many people, this is the pinnacle of fame for music. One may, however, think otherwise without an excess of abnormality.

[1] Giovanni Pierluigi (Palestrina), the celebrated Italian composer of church music, born Palestrina, 1524; died 1594.

[2] Tomaso Ludovico da Vittoria, born probably at Airla about 1540, died probably at Madrid about 1608; ranked as a composer of church music second only to Palestrina.

[3] Orlandus Lassus (di Lasso), born about 1520; died Munich, 1594: was the last great composer of the early Netherland School, ranking, as far as his *Penitential Psalms* are concerned, with Palestrina.

[4] The *Valkyrie*, Act I.

I should add that this conception of ornament has vanished completely; music has been successfully domesticated. It has become a family matter; and when a family does not know what to do with a child—since the brilliant profession of engineering is beginning to be terribly overcrowded—they have him taught music and there is one more mediocrity. If sometimes this or that man of genius tries to escape the galling yoke of tradition, care is taken to swamp him with ridicule; so the poor man of genius elects to die very young, this being the sole performance for which he will get an appreciative audience.

VII   The Opera

Everybody knows our national Opera House, at least by repute. I can assure you from painful experience that it has not changed. A stranger would take it for a railway station and, once inside, would mistake it for a Turkish bath.

They continue to produce curious noises which the people who pay call music, but there is no need to believe them implicitly.

By special permission and a State subsidy this theatre may produce anything; it matters so little what, that elaborately luxurious *loges à salons* have been installed, so-called because they are the most convenient places for not hearing anything of the music: they are the last *salons* where conversation still takes place.

By this I do not mean to cast any reflection upon the ability of the directors, so sure am I that the best of good intentions are shattered against a solid and solemn wall of obstinate officialdom, impenetrable by any revealing light. There will never be any change short of a revolution, although revolutionaries do not always give consideration to such institutions. We might hope for a fire, if fire were not too indiscriminating in its effects on undoubtedly innocent persons.

Much however might be done if the busy apathy of the place were shaken off. Why have we not long ago been given

the whole of *The Ring?* In the first place this would have en-
abled us to get rid of it, and Bayreuth pilgrims could no longer
bore us with their stories. To produce *The Meistersingers* is
good; *Tristan and Isolde* is better, for the entrancing spirit of
Chopin inspires the swirl and passion of the music.

Without prejudice to our grievances, let us consider how
far the Opera has served to develop dramatic music in France.

Much of Reyer[1] has been performed. The reasons of his
success seem to me peculiar. Some people look at landscapes
with the indifference of cattle; and the same people listen to
music with cotton-wool in their ears.

Saint-Saëns composed operas with the impenitence of a
convinced symphonist. Is that where the future will look for
the true reasons for continuing to admire him?

Massenet seems to have been the victim of the fluttering
fans of his fair hearers, who flirted them so long. to his glory;
he yearned to reserve for himself the beating of those perfumed
wings; unfortunately he might as well have tried to tame a cloud
of butterflies. Perhaps he only lacked patience and under-
valued silence. His influence on contemporary music is obvious,
but admitted grudgingly by certain persons who owe much to
him, though they have the hypocrisy and ingratitude to deny it.

Among too many stupid ballets Lalo's *Namouna*[2] is something of a masterpiece. Who knows what dumb hatred has
buried it so deeply that we never hear of it now? What a loss
to music!

There has been throughout no attempt at anything really
new; nothing but a kind of humming of machinery, a continual reiteration. It might be said that when music enters the
Opera it dons a prescribed uniform, like a convict; moreover
at the Opera music assumes the pompous proportions of the
building, vying with the well-known great staircase which,
through an error in the perspective or too much detail, in fact
appears insignificant.

Why should not the Opera be administered by a council of

---

1 See Note 3, p. 6.
2 Edouard Victor Antonine Lalo, born Lille, 1823; died Paris, 1892.
Among his best-known works are *Le Roi d'Ys, La Symphonie Espagnole*
and *Namouna*.

people too rich to trouble about sound speculations, but likely to take pride in having plenty of money for the production of great works? It is only a question of judgment and selection.

Then, why not have a perfectly freé and independent director, whose business would be, first, to know all about art movements and, secondly, to ensure in advance a programme of classical and carefully-chosen works? When Wagner's operas are given, why not invite Richter to conduct the orchestra? I merely take this as an example. This would provide an attraction for the public, as well as the certainty of a fine performance. I do not wish to labour the point, but what I suggest is no innovation, since such a scheme is, in effect, the principle of Covent Garden, where the performances are in every respect excellent. It is lamentable that we cannot do better, if not equally well, at the Opera. Even if it be a question of money I refuse to agree.

To sum up, the important thing is to perform a great deal of music and not to yield to the wilful indifference of the public.

Certain artists have a serious responsibility for this indifference; they know how to strive just long enough to gain a footing in the musical marketplace, but the sale of their goods once assured they retire promptly, seeming to apologise to the public for the trouble it has taken to admit them. Resolutely turning their backs on their youth they are lulled to sleep by success. They are never able to rise to a fame happily reserved for men whose lives, consecrated to the search for a world of ever-renewed sensations and forms, have ended in the joyous confidence of a noble task accomplished. Such men have obtained what may be termed a "last-night" success—if "success" be not too mean a word for what is glory. I am not so bold as to demand that the Opera should ever assist the latter, but it need not exclusively support the former. My aim has been to prove that the wrongs are not all on one side.

VIII   *Nikisch*

On Sunday the overpowering glare of the sun seemed to make it unthinkable to listen to music. The

Berlin Philharmonic Orchestra, conducted by Nikisch,[1] took the opportunity of giving its first concert. I hope that God will forgive my having gone back on my resolutions and that others more fortunate paid homage to the grass generously spread by Him for the reception of sausage skins and the logical development of idylls.

All the well-known and attentive ears that Paris boasts were there, and particularly the dear wonderful ladies! This is the best kind of audience for any one who knows how to make use of it. Almost all that is required to rouse its enthusiasm is a graceful attitude or a romantically waved lock of hair.

Nikisch has the pose and the lock, but fortunately he has more solid qualities too. Moreover, he has his orchestra marvellously in hand and one seems to be in the presence of men whose sole aim is the serious production of music: for they are staid and unaffected like the figures in a primitive fresco—quite a touching novelty.

Nikisch is an unique virtuoso, so much so that his virtuosity seems to make him forget the claims of good taste! I would take as an example his performance of the *Tannhäuser* overture, in which he forces the trombones to a *portamento* suitable at best to the stout lady responsible for the sentimental ditties at the *Casino de Suresnes* and in which he stresses the horns at points where there is no particular reason for bringing them into prominence. These are effects without any appreciable causes and are amazing in a musician as experienced as Nikisch shows himself at all other times. At an earlier period he had proved his unique gifts in Richard Strauss' *The Merry Pranks of Till Eulenspiegel*. This piece might almost be called, "An hour of original music in a lunatic asylum." The clarinets leap in frenzied curves, the trumpets everlastingly choke and the horns, forestalling a latent sneeze, hasten to rejoin: "God bless you!" while a big drum goes boom! boom! apparently emphasizing the antics of the clowns. One wants either to shout with laughter or to shriek with pain. Then follows the startling discovery that everything is in the right place; for, if the double-basses blew down their bows and the trombones fiddled on their brass tubes with

---

1 Arthur Nikisch, one of the foremost of the world's conductors, born 1855, on Baron Sina's estate in Hungary; died 1922.

an imaginary bow, or if Nikisch perched himself on the knee
of a programme seller, it would not be in the least surprising.
Meanwhile there is no gainsaying the fact that genius is shown
at times in this work, above all in the amazing orchestral assurance, the mad rhythm that sweeps us along from beginning
to end and forces us to share in all the hero's merry pranks.
Nikisch conducted this ordered tumult with astounding coolness
and the ovation which greeted both his orchestra and himself
was eminently justified.

During the performance of Schubert's *Unfinished Sym-
phony*[1] a flock of sparrows fluttered to the windows of the *Cirque*[2]
and twittered pleasantly. Nikisch had the grace not to demand
the expulsion of these impertinent melomaniacs, who were
probably drunk with the ether or perhaps were merely innocent
critics of a symphony which cannot decide once and for all
to remain unfinished.

IX   *Massenet*

I should like to try to give, not a por-
trait of Massenet,[3] but rather some indication of the mental
attitude he aimed at conveying through his music; besides, the
incidents or foibles that constitute the life of a man must be
posthumous to have genuine interest.

Music was never for Massenet the cosmic voice heard by
Bach and Beethoven: to him it was rather a delightful avocation.

Look at the long list of his works. You will note a constant
preoccupation which directs his advance like the hand of fate.
It makes him rediscover in his last opera, *Grisélidis*, some of the
escapades of one of his youthful works, *Eve*. Is this not due to
a kind of mysterious and irresistible fate which explains Massenet's untiring curiosity in seeking in music the data for the
history of the feminine soul? Here are all or nearly all the

---

1 The eighth of Schubert's ten Symphonies in B minor, the two
movements of which are among his posthumous works.

2 *Le Cirque d'Eté*, where the Lamoureux Concerts take place. See
Note 1, p. 12.

3 See Note 2, p. 10.

women's faces which have been the stuff of so many dreams! The smile of a Manon in a panniered gown is born again on the lips of a modern Sappho, again to make men weep! The knife of the woman of Navarre matches the pistol of the conscienceless Charlotte. (Cf. *Werther*.)

On the other hand, we know how vibrant his music is with thrills, transports and would-be eternal embraces. The harmonies are like enlacing arms, the melodies are the necks we kiss; we gaze into women's eyes to learn at any cost what lies behind. Philosophers and robust people assert that nothing lies behind; but that this does not entirely exclude a contrary opinion the example of Massenet proves, at least in melody; to this preoccupation moreover he owes the position he holds in contemporary art—which we secretly envy him, a fact that makes it probable that it is not to be despised.

Fortune, being a woman, certainly ought to treat Massenet kindly and even on occasions to be unfaithful to him; and in this she has not failed. At one time, owing to his great success, it was correct to imitate his melodious fancies; then, suddenly, those who had so calmly plagiarised him turned violently against him.

He was reproached with having shown excessive sympathy for Mascagni and not enough worship of Wagner. This reproach is as false as it is inadmissible. Massenet continued heroically to court the approbation of his feminine admirers as before. I confess I cannot understand why it is any better to please old cosmopolitan Wagnerian ladies than scented young ones, even though they do not play the piano very well. In short, he was right. He can only seriously be reproached with his infidelities to Manon. He had discovered a suitable form for his flirtatious inclinations; and he should not have tried to impose them on the Opera. No one flirts at the Opera; for there they shriek unintelligible words at the top of their voices and if any vows are exchanged it is with the approval of the trombones. Logically, the finer shades of sentiment must be lost in the resulting din. Massenet surely would have been wiser to go on expressing his genius in delicate colours and whispering melodies and in light airy structures. The refinements of art would not thereby have been excluded; they would have been more exquisite, that is all. There is no lack, however, of musicians who grasp music with outstretched arms while the trumpets blare. Why increase the number uselessly? And why encourage an increase of the taste for tedious music which comes to us from the neo-Wagnerians and which might well favour us by returning to the country of its origin?

Massenet, by reason of his unique gifts and his facility, might have opposed considerable influence to that deplorable movement. It is not always best to do in Rome as the Romans do: a piece of advice which I think the least subtle of his fair hearers might have given him.

Massenet was the most truly loved of all contemporary musicians. It is, indeed, to that very love that he owes the unique standing which he still has in the musical world.

His brethren could not readily forgive this power of pleasing which, strictly speaking, is a gift. It must be admitted that this gift is not indispensable, particularly in art; to take but one example, Bach never "pleased" in the sense of the word as applied to Massenet. Has one ever heard of young milliners humming *The Passion according to St. Matthew?* I do not think so. But everyone knows that they wake in the morning and sing *Manon* or *Werther.* Make no mistake: this is a delightful kind of fame, the secret envy of many of those great purists, who can only warm their hands at the somewhat pallid flame of the approbation of the elect.

Massenet amply succeeded in what he set out to do, a fact which caused some to believe that they were taking their revenge by calling him—*sotto voce*—Paul Delmet's[1] best pupil. That is merely a joke in the worst possible taste. He has been much imitated abroad as well as at home.

To endeavour to overthrow those whom they imitate is the first principle of wisdom with certain artists, who call such reprehensible methods the struggle for art. This hackneyed phrase is somewhat disingenuous and has, moreover, the defect of likening art to a kind of sport.

In art the struggle is more often against oneself alone and victories so achieved are perhaps the finest. By a curious irony, however, we are afraid of a victory over ourselves, and

[1] A writer of ballad music, born and died Paris, 1862-1904.

it seems preferable to be quietly merged in the public or to imitate our friends, which amounts to the same thing.

In the time of Napoleon, every French mother hoped that her son would be another Napoleon. The game of war frustrated most of those dreams. Besides, there are such things as unique destinies. Such, in its own class, is the destiny of Massenet.

X *Open-air Music*

It is certain that in France there is no love left to-day for street-organs. It is only once a year at beflagged celebrations of the Fourteenth of July, or in vacant lots more suited to the mutterings of hooligans than to the fugitive dreams of melomaniacs, that they still venture to grind out melancholy strains from their husky pipes.

Ought we to regret this fact and conclude that there is a decline in the standard of music in France today? My business is neither to make any such assertion nor to blame anyone.

Nevertheless, M. Gavioli, the famous maker of these instruments, does not seem quite to have done his duty. Is it really enough to have recorded during recent years the *Cavalleria Rusticana Intermezzo*, the *Valse Bleue* and a few other masterpieces? Why so limited a programme? Might he not have paid some attention to the need for popularity of our notable contemporaries? Is there not a mass of music now mouldering away in the programmes of Sunday concerts, the revival of which on the street-organ would be delightful, if M. Gavioli were not so hopelessly insensible to the demands of his age? Be modern, sir, we implore you! Do not allow negro kings to monopolise the charms of a perfect instrument. Know that the Shah of Persia owns an electric organ which plays the Prelude to *Parsifal* with the utmost verisimilitude. If you think that these performances in the harems do Wagner justice, you are wrong. Despite his taste for the mysterious, this particular example goes a little too far, you will admit. Besides, did he not declare again and again that he could only be understood in France? May we hope that you will eventually see where your duty lies? The Opera does not shrink from playing *Pagliacci;* shrink then no longer from making street-organs worthy to perform *The Ring.*

As a matter of fact the apparent futility of these reflections arises because people only worry about the banality of things; they deplore them, but never remedy them. To those who find this defence of the street-organ ridiculous, the answer is that we are not referring to the pleasures of the dilettante, but to the duty of dealing with the mediocrity of the herd mind.

Without defending the frequenters of *cafés-concerts* any more than those of the *Concerts Lamoureux*, we must admit that they are both right in their special planes. There are others who can only be moved by open-air music, which, as performed in these days, is certainly the best imaginable educator of mediocrity.

In short, why have the amenities of squares and promenades remained the monopoly of military bands? I know quite well that there is the music of the Republican Guard,[1] but that is on a higher plane—it is practically an instrument of diplomacy.

I should like to imagine simpler entertainments in greater harmony with natural scenery. Is not military music an anodyne for the rigours of the march and a source of joy in the streets? It sums up the patriotism that thrills the hearts of each one of us; it is the link between the little pastry-cook with his dreams and the old gentleman who thinks of Alsace-Lorraine and never speaks of it. Never would the idea occur to anyone to rob that music of its noble privilege; but, among the trees, it is like the strident notes of some huge gramophone.

We can imagine a great orchestra, further strengthened by human voices—not a choral society, thank you! Here is the germ of a kind of music composed especially for the open air, on broad lines, with bold vocal and instrumental effects, which would sport and skim among the tree-tops in the sunshine and fresh air. Harmonies which would seem out of place in an enclosed concert room would be in their true environment here. One might even discover the means of escape from the fads about form and the arbitrarily fixed tone values which so awkwardly encumber music.

I should add that I do not suggest the "wholesale" but

1 The Garde républicaine, a section of the Gendarmerie. This famous French military band visited England a few years ago.

the "grand" plan; I do not suggest plaguing the echoes to repeat great masses of sound, but using them to prolong an harmonic dream in the soul of the crowd. The murmuring of the breeze would be mystically mingled with the rustling of the leaves and the scent of the flowers, since music can unite all of them in a harmony so completely natural that it seems to become one with them. The tall peaceful trees would be like the pipes of a great organ, and would lend their branches to clusters of children, who would be taught the charming rounds of long ago, to which the feeble tunes which disgrace the towns and gardens of to-day are such poor successors.

We might even rediscover that counterpoint, which we have made an academic study, yet which, in the hands of the old masters of the French Renaissance, had something of laughter.

I confess that if this happened I could bear the banishment of the street-organ without a tear; but I fear that music will continue to suggest closed windows.

XI   Recollections

The recent foggy weather has made me think of London and of the charming play, *A Midsummer Night's Dream*, whose true and more poetic title would be *A Dream of St. John's Eve*, the shortest night of the year. A warm night, radiant with stars whose short-lived enchantment lies between a lingering twilight and an impatient dawn. A dream night whose span is but a single dream. Nor was Oberon, the fairy king, saved from a touch of gracious jealousy by his cares as master of the midnight revels; he even found time to test the too-frail virtue of Titania with the aid of Puck, or Robin Goodfellow, that merry reveller of the night, that mischievous rascal, that sweet player of pranks, whose aid one could invoke by calling him "Hobgoblin and sweet Puck."

But I am especially reminded of a man, now nearly forgotten, at least in the theatre. I saw him trudging along the London streets, his body consumed by the vivid light that was in him and in his face that radiance peculiar to those who have known beauty. On he went, sustained by the feverish desire to postpone death until he had heard that posthumous work born of the fiery pangs of his ebbing life: By what miracle did he revive in it that wild passion, that rhythm of romance, which had won such immediate recognition for his youthful genius? No one will ever know.

His work had a sort of dreamy melancholy, characteristic of his time, though never marred by the crude German moonshine in which nearly all his contemporaries were bathed.

He was perhaps the first to face the problem of establishing the due relationship of the infinite spirit of nature to the finite spirit of the individual. At all events he utilised the legend, feeling that thus music would find its natural course. For music, and music alone, has the power of evoking at will imaginary scenes —that real yet elusive world which gives birth in secret to the mystic poetry of the night and the thousand nameless sounds of the leaves caressed by the moonlight.

He was master of every known means of interpreting the fantastic through music. Even in our own days, rich as they are in the science of orchestration, few have surpassed him. If he attached too much importance to the flourish and the *coloratura* we must not forget that he married a singer. Probably he adored her. It is a sentimental reason, yet none the worse for that; particularly so because his taste for tying true lovers' knots with graceful semi-quavers did not hinder him time and again from using simple and beautiful language free from useless verbiage. This man—have you not all recognized him? was Charles-Marie Weber.[1] The opera, the final effort of his genius, was *Oberon,* first performed in London. You see I had excellent reasons for thinking of that city.

Some years earlier he had succeeded in getting the *Freischütz* produced at Berlin, and afterwards *Euryanthe.* That is the reason for his becoming the father of that romantic school to which we owe Berlioz,[2] who is so enamoured of the romance of colour

[1] Caroline Brandt, a young actress and singer, married Karl Maria Friedrich Ernst von Weber in 1817; the famous composer was born Entin, Oldenburg, in 1786; and died London, 1826.

[2] Hector Berlioz, born Côte-Saint-André, Isère, 1803; died Paris, 1869; developed the resources of the orchestra to an enormous extent, and was the first to employ large masses of musicians and singers to produce big tonal effects. Among his best-known works are *Benvenuto Cellini* and *La Damnation de Faust.*

that he sometimes forgets music, Wagner, the great master sym-
bolist, and, nearer to our own time, Richard Strauss,[1] whose
imagination seems created for romanticism. Weber may be
proud of such descendants and the glory of the offspring of
his genius may console him for the fact that scarcely anything but
the overtures of the above works are ever performed.

XII   Rameau

Charles Bordes[2] is famous throughout
the entire world for the best of all possible reasons. In the first
place he is an accomplished musician in every sense of the word;
in the second place he has the inspiration of those fiery mis-
sionaries of old times whose spirit shone out in the face of difficulties. It is admittedly less dangerous to preach Palestrina to
the crowds than the Gospel to savages; yet one may meet with
the same hostility—the difference is only in the penalty: in the
one case it is scalping, in the other yawning.

Charles Bordes, appointed choir-master at *Saint Gervais
de Paris*, inaugurated the series of "Holy Weeks of Saint Gervais," the success of which was so considerable as to alarm the
church dignitaries who thought, quite wrongly, that it distracted
the attention of the faithful. He who reigns in heaven above,
however, gave no sign of being shocked.

This caused Bordes to found the *Association des Chanteurs
de Saint Gervais* for performing old choral music. From that
moment dates his incessant craving for propaganda, for there
is no town in which this society has not preached its gospel.
It would not be surprising if one day Bordes were to lead his
associates to Sirius or Aldebaran.

He was also the promoter of the *Schola Cantorum,* originally

1 See Note 2, p. 21.
2 Charles Bordes, born Vouvray-sur-Loire, 1863; died 1909; founded
the now world-famous choir, *Les Chanteurs de St. Gervais* in 1890 while
organist at the Paris church of that name. In 1894 he founded with Guil-
mant and d'Indy the *Schola Cantorum,* whose object was to raise the
standard of music in French churches by a return to plain song, the
old masters, etc.

founded for the restoration of church music, but subsequently extending its programme until it became a kind of musical High School.

It was there that we heard recently the first two acts of *Castor and Pollux*. Rameau[1] to many people is the author of nothing but the celebrated *Rigaudon* from *Dardanus*.

Here is an excellent example of the peculiar temperament of the French which impels them to adopt art formulas as eagerly as they adopt fashions in clothes which bear no relation to their native genius.

Gluck's[2] influence on French music is recognized, an influence only possible through the intervention of the Dauphine, Marie-Antoinette, an Austrian—a curious analogy to the case of Wagner, who owed the production of *Tannhäuser* in Paris to the influence of Mme. de Metternich, also an Austrian. Yet Gluck's genius is deeply rooted in the work of Rameau. *Castor and Pollux* is an epitome of preliminary sketches developed later by Gluck. Considerable evidence can be adduced for the statement that Gluck was only able to supplant Rameau on the French stage by assimilating Rameau's finest creations and making them his own. To what does the Gluck tradition owe its survival? The false and pompous treatment of recitative is enough, but there is also his habit of rudely interrupting the action, as, for example, where Orpheus, having lost his Eurydice, sings a song which does not precisely indicate a very mournful state of mind. But because it is Gluck we bend the knee. Rameau need only have changed his nationality—that was his mistake.

We have, however, in Rameau's work a pure French' tradition full of charming and tender delicacy, well balanced, strictly declamatory in recitative and without any affection of German profundity or over-emphasis or impatient explanation, as if to say: "You are a collection of utter idiots who understand

---

[1] Jean Philippe Rameau, born Dijon, 1683, died 1768; wrote a number of works on the theory of music; among his best-known compositions are *Hippolyte et Aricie, Castor et Pollux, Le Temple de la Gloire.*

[2] Christoph Willibald von Gluck, born Weidenwang in the Upper Palatinate, 1714, died Vienna, 1787; revolutionised the opera by making the music support the poetry without interrupting the action. Among his best-known works are the operas *Alceste, Iphigénie en Aulide, Orphée et Eurydice, Iphigénie en Tauride.*

nothing unless you are first compelled to believe that the moon is made of green cheese." We may, however, regret that French music should so long have followed a course treacherously leading it away from that clarity of expression, that terse and condensed form, which is the peculiar and significant quality of the French genius. I know quite well the theory of free trade in art and its valuable results; but this does not excuse us from having so completely forgotten the tradition that permeates Rameau's work, a tradition filled with far-reaching, almost unparalleled discoveries.

To return to *Castor and Pollux*. The scene is the burial-place of the Kings of Sparta. After an overture, only required to allow time for the silken folds of the panniered dresses to be spread out, the wailing voices of a chorus solemnising the obsequies of Castor are heard. At once we breathe an atmosphere of tragedy which yet remains human. We are not so much conscious of the peplum and of the helmet as of people weeping as we might weep ourselves. Then Talaïra, Castor's love, enters and utters the sweetest, most touching lament that ever sprang from a loving heart. Pollux appears at the head of his warriors, who have avenged the outrage on Castor. Then the chorus and a martial ballet superb in its forceful rhythm, slashed now and again with a blare of trumpets, end the first act.

The second act introduces us to the fore-court of Jupiter's temple, where all is prepared for a sacrifice; and this is a sheer marvel; I wish I could describe it in its entirety. The aria of Pollux, "Nature, love, who share my fate," has so personal a touch, such freshness of construction, that time and space vanish, and Rameau seems to be a contemporary to whom we render our homage on leaving. How moving it is!

Then follows the scene in which Pollux and Talaïra sacrifice their great love to the will of the gods; the entrance of Jupiter's High Priest; the appearance of Jupiter himself seated on a throne of glory, so royally gentle and compassionate of the human sorrow of Pollux, a poor mortal whom he, the chief òf the gods, could crush at will—as I said, it ought to be described in its entirety.

And then the last scene of the act. Hebe leads in the dance the Celestial Pleasures whose hands are filled with garlands for the capture of Pollux. Jupiter has ordained the enchantments of this scene in order to wean Pollux from his desire for death. Never before has so calm and soothing an appeal to the senses been so perfectly rendered, so luminous is its play in the supernatural atmosphere that all the Spartan strength of Pollux is needed to escape its spell and remember Castor. I myself had forgotten him for the moment.

In conclusion we must not fail to mention the exquisite grace of the music, a grace which never descends to affectation or to meritricious beauty. Has such music been ousted by a taste for "the pretty," or by our preference for Byzantine craftsmanship?

XIII   Beethoven

Last Sunday was an irresistibly beautiful day. The first sunshine of spring seemed to preclude all idea of listening to music; it was weather to bring the swallows back again.

Weingartner[1] seized the opportunity to conduct the orchestra of the *Concerts Lamoureux*.[2] No one is perfect!

He first conducted the *Pastoral Symphony*[3] with the care of a conscientious gardener. He tidied it so neatly as to produce the illusion of a meticulously finished landscape in which the gently undulating hills are made of plush at ten francs the yard and the foliage is crimped with curling-tongs.

The popularity of the *Pastoral Symphony* is due to the widespread misunderstanding that exists between Man and Nature. Consider the scene on the banks of the stream: a stream to which it appears the oxen come to drink, so at least the bassoons would have us suppose; to say nothing of the wooden nightingale and the Swiss cuckoo-clock, more representative of the artistry of M. de Vaucanson[4] than of genuine Nature. It is

1 See Note 1, p. 21.
2 See Note 1, p. 12.
3 Beethoven's 6th Symphony in F major, op. 68.
4 Jacques de Vaucanson, 1709-1782, a mechanician of Grenoble; his automata *The Duck* and *The Flute Player* are famous.

unnecessarily imitative and the interpretation is entirely arbitrary.

How much more profound an interpretation of the beauty of a landscape do we find in other passages in the great Master, because, instead of an exact imitation, there is an emotional interpretation of what is invisible in Nature. Can the mystery of a forest be expressed by measuring the height of the trees? Is it not rather its fathomless depths that stir the imagination?

In this symphony Beethoven inaugurates an epoch when Nature was seen only through the pages of books. This is proved by the storm, a part of this same symphony, where the terror of man and Nature is draped in the folds of the cloak of romanticism amid the rumblings of rather disarming thunder.

It would be absurd to imagine that I am wanting in respect for Beethoven; yet a musician of his genius may be deceived more completely than another. No man is bound to write nothing but masterpieces; and, if the *Pastoral Symphony* is so regarded, the expression must be weakened as a description of the other symphonies. That is all I mean.

Then Weingartner conducted an orchestral fantasy by Chevillard[1]; in which the most extraordinary orchestration lends itself to a highly personal method of developing his ideas. A gentleman who was extremely fond of music furiously expressed his dislike of the fantasy by whistling on a key. This was excessively stupid. Could anyone tell whether the said gentleman was criticising Weingartner's manner of conducting or the composer's music? One reason is that the key is not an instrument of warfare, but a domestic article. Monsieur Croche always preferred the butcher-boys' elegant method of whistling with their fingers: it is louder. Perhaps the gentleman is still young enough to learn this art!

Weingartner recovered ground by conducting Liszt's *Mazeppa* magnificently. This symphonic poem is full of the worst faults, occasionally descending even to the commonplace; yet the stormy passion that rages throughout captures us at last so completely that we are content to accept it without further reasoning. We may affect an air of contempt on leaving, because that is pleasant—though it is sheer hypocrisy. The undeniable

1 See Note 1, p. 12.

beauty of Liszt's work arises, I believe, from the fact that his love of music excluded every other kind of emotion. If sometimes he gets on easy terms with it and frankly takes it on his knee, this surely is no worse than the stilted manner of those who behave as though they were being introduced to it for the first time; very polite, but rather dull. Liszt's genius is often disordered and feverish, but that is better than rigid perfection, even in white gloves.

Weingartner's personal appearance suggests at the first glance a new knife. His gestures have a kind of angular grace; then suddenly the imperious movement of his arms seems to compel the trombones to bellow and to drive the cymbals to frenzy. It is most impressive and verges on the miraculous; the enthusiasm of the audience knows no bounds.

XIV   The People's Theatre

For some time now there has been a widespread movement for developing in the soul of the people a taste for the arts in general and for music in particular. I quote as examples the *Conservatoire de Mimi Pinson*,[1] where Gustave Charpentier practises the theories dear to his youthful genius. This enables him to give a taste for freedom in art as well as in life to girls whose æsthetic outlook has hitherto been bounded on the north by Delmet[2] and on the south by Decourcelle.[3] Now they know the names of Gluck and Bruneau[4]; and their pretty tapering fingers, so skilled in tying bows, caress Lyon's chromatic harp.[5] They will certainly grow into charming

---

1 Gustave Charpentier, born Dieuze, 1860; best known as the composer of the opera *Louise*. In 1900 he founded the *Conservatoire populaire de Mimi Pinson* to give free courses in popular music and classical dancing.

2 See Note p. 30.

3 Adrien Decourcelle, the dramatic writer, born Paris, 1821; died Etretat, 1892; wrote the famous drama *Jenny l'Ouvrière*.

4 Louis Charles Bonaventure Alfred Bruneau; born Paris, 1857; composed a number of operas to libretti by Zola.

5 The chromatic harp of Pleyel improved and simplified by Gustave Lyon in 1903.

young women instead of the silly nonentities they were otherwise likely to become.

The fame of *Les Noces de Jeanette*[1] is perishing too; and as for *La Dame Blanche*,[2] she is at death's door.

> *Chevaliers félons et méchants*
> *Qui tramez complots malfaisants . . .*

you need no longer trouble yourselves to guard against that old lady. I pass over the songs where Mignon laments her native land and other young persons their "faded posies"; for they are in the coolest of thy lakes, O Norway![3]

Then we have the *Théâtre-roulotte*[4] of Catulle Mendès, a delightful idea, also what is known as *Thirty Years of the Stage,* immortalised by A. Bernheim, who carries the solemnity of the *Comédie Française* into the most incongruous surroundings.

In my humble way I have assisted in endeavours to spread art among the people; and I confess that I have only the memory of deep depression. Usually those who make themselves responsible for these attempts assume a sort of patronising goodwill of which the poor victims perfectly appreciate the spuriousness and affectation. They certainly make up their minds to laugh or cry to order. In any case it is not genuine. An instinctive feeling of envy hovers vaguely over this vision of luxury imported

---

1 Light opera composed by Victor Massé in 1853; the libretto is by Barbier and Carré.

2 Light opera composed by Boieldieu in 1825; the libretto is by Scribe. The quotation "Chevaliers félons," etc., is from this work.

3 Reference would appear to be made here to Grieg.

4 In 1887 M. Ritt, director of the Opera at Paris, proposed to the Minister of Fine Arts a scheme for the formation of a Popular Theatre, but owing to lack of funds his project was never realized. Adrien Bernheim, born 1861, was General Inspector and Government Commissioner of the subsidised theatres. He founded in 1902 l'Œuvre Française des Trente Ans de Théâtre, which was a fund to help all those directly or indirectly connected with the theatre who after thirty years of work were ill or in want. The fund was formed from the proceeds of a series of dramatic and operatic performances given in the suburban theatres by the companies of the large subsidised theatres. Bernheim hoped by these means to lay the foundations of a Popular Theatre, as he was convinced it was the most workable form it could take; he considered Catulle Mendès' idea of a *théâtre-roulotte,* or caravan theatre, entirely impracticable. Bernheim's project was in fact recognized in the French Chamber shortly after its inception as the basis of a Popular Theatre.

for a moment into their dismal lives; the women appraise the frocks with forced smiles; the men make comparisons, feel discontented and dream of impossible joys; others regret their sixpences, and all go home sadly to eat their soup which is sure to be spoiled that night—flavoured just a little, I think, with tears.

I can well appreciate the good motives underlying these social efforts and inspired enthusiasms. Nothing is more exciting than to act the part of a little Buddha with an egg and two glasses of water a day and to give all else to the poor; to indulge in endless reveries on the origin of the universe and the all-pervading godhead, hotchpotches of *natura naturans* and a delicious confusion of the Ego and the Non-Ego and its reabsorption into the Universal Soul. It is all very pretty and useful in conversation; but unhappily it has not an ounce of practical value and sometimes even leads to dangerous results.

If it is really a good thing to provide performances for the people, there should be a definite idea as to the character of such performances. Perhaps it would be best to revive the ancient games of the Roman imperial circus. We have our Zoological Gardens which would feel bound to lend their finest inmates; the old lions who yawn from the sheer boredom of gazing at everlasting soldier boys and nurse maids, would at once recover their natural ferocity. Would it be more difficult to find art enthusiasts devoted enough to be the victims? After all, one never knows. If the price is high enough—

But I am afraid we must give that up and return to the People's Theatre. All needs are supposed to have been met by the production of the old repertory plays or antique dramas breathless with romanticism.

That is not a very brilliant effort! What we must discover, it seems to me, is a form of art, suited both in its essence and in its staging to the greatest possible number. I do not here pretend to be axiomatic, but why not remember the Greeks?

Do we not find in Euripides, Sophocles and Æschylus the mighty impulses of humanity simply portrayed with such natural tragedy of effects that they are at once intelligible to the least enlightened and to the least cultured minds? For example, conceive of a performance of the *Agamemnon* of Æschylus which has been so admirably translated by Paul Claudel.[1]

Would not this be nearer to the heart of the people than all the psychological or fashionable subtleties of our present-day repertory? When it is a question of making people forget their domestic cares, nothing can be too sublime; if the aim be to snatch them away from life, to give them exact interpretations of it, however excellent, must be harmful.

This brings me to mention the People's Opera, a recent scheme, the realisation of which presents the most serious difficulties. At a pinch one might discover a comic actor; the old Free Theatre affords a striking example of this; but as yet we have not gone far enough with the science of suggestion to compel the first passer-by to play the double-bass. Whether it seems so or not, this little fact is extremely important. An opera needs an orchestra and where shall we find it? Singers are necessary and a chorus and so on. What shall be performed? Works from the old-fashioned repertory, as usual? Something like *La Juive*[2] or a musty *Muette de Portici*?[3]

If for the moment we abandon the belief in a voyage to Utopia, still there is a method of settling the matter by combining the People's Theatre with the People's Opera—in fact, as I wrote above, by reverting to the dramatic methods of the ancient Greeks. Let us rediscover Tragedy, strengthening its primitive musical setting by means of the infinite resources of the modern orchestra and a chorus of innumerable voices; let us remember at the same time how effective is the combination of pantomime and dance accompanied by the fullest possible development of lighting required for a vast audience. We could glean valuable hints for this from the entertainments arranged by the Javanese princes, where the fascination of speech without words, that is to say of pantomime, almost attains perfection, since it is rendered by action and not by formulas. The trouble about our theatre is that we have tried to confine it to the intellectual element alone.

---

[1] Paul Claudel, diplomatist and literary man, born Villeneuve-sur-Feu, 1868.

[2] Opera by Halévy, 1835, libretto by Scribe.

[3] Opera by Auber, 1828, libretto by Scribe and Delavigne.

Such a change would be so successful that we should find it impossible to bear anything else. Paris would become a centre to which pilgrims in search of beauty would flock from all over the world. To sum up, we must have large ideas. No more petty undertakings based on disingenuous theorising! Since it is absolutely necessary to build a special theatre, as no existing one would be suitable, let the Municipal Council and the State try to come to terms—they need not make a habit of it.

It must not be a theatre in which the gilding catches the eye unpleasantly, but a bright, cheerful house, attractive to everyone. I need not emphasise the necessity for completely free seats; if necessary let a loan be raised. There could never be one for a more lofty or strictly patriotic object.

We must never forget that there is a law of beauty! In spite of isolated protests we seem to be in danger of forgetting it. The thousand-headed monster mediocrity has so many worshippers in the modern artistic associations.

XV   Richard Strauss

Richard Strauss,[1] who recently conducted the orchestra at the *Concerts Lamoureux,* is no relation to *The Blue Danube*:[2] he was born at Munich in 1864, where his father was a musician in the Royal Household. He is practically the only original composer in modern Germany; his remarkable technique in the art of handling an orchestra allies him to Liszt, while his desire to found his music on literature allies him to Berlioz; witness the titles of his symphonic poems, *Don Quixote, Thus Spake Zarathustra, The Merry Pranks of Till Eulenspiegel.* As a matter of fact the art of Richard Strauss is not invariably so exclusively interpretative; but he undoubtedly thinks in colour-pictures and he seems to draw the line of his ideas by means of the orchestra. This is no commonplace method and few people have adopted it. Richard Strauss, moreover, develops

[1] See Note 2, p. 21.

[2] The famous waltz *An der schönen blauen Donau,* written by the famous composer and conductor of dance music, Johann Strauss, born Vienna, 1825, died 1899.

it along peculiarly personal lines; it is no longer the rigid and architectural method of Bach or Beethoven, but the working out of a scheme of rhythmic colours; he combines with the utmost assurance the most wildly discordant notes, quite regardless of their possibly painful effect as long as they satisfy his demand that they should live.

All these characteristics reach a pitch of frenzy in the *Heldenleben,* the symphonic poem of which Richard Strauss here gave the second performance in Paris. One may not care for certain experiments which border on the commonplace or for a kind of tortured Italianism; but after a minute or two one is captured first by the tremendous versatility of his orchestration, then by the frenzied energy which carries one with him for as long as he chooses; the hearer is no longer master of his emotions, he does not even notice that this symphonic poem exceeds the limits that our patience usually allows to such compositions.

Once again, it is a book of pictures, or even a cinematograph. But one must admit that the man who composed such a work at so continuously high a pressure is very nearly a genius.

He began by giving *Italy,* a symphonic fantasy in four parts— an early work, I believe—where the future originality of Strauss is already discernible. The elaboration seemed to me a trifle long and stereotyped. But the third part, *In the Bay of Sorrento,* is very beautiful in colour. Then came a love scene from *Feuersnot,* his last opera. This suffered considerably through being detached from its context; and, since the programme gave no explanation, its relation to the rest was wholly incomprehensible. An episode which evoked such orchestral torrents seemed somewhat formidable for a love scene! It is probable that in the opera the torrent is justified. Perhaps it may afford an opportunity for the opera houses to produce something new; for I do not think they can pretend to teach us anything at all by producing the modern operas of Young Italy.

Richard Strauss has no wild lock of hair, no epileptic gestures. He is tall and has the free and determined bearing of those great explorers who journey among savage tribes with a smile on their lips. Perhaps this sort of bearing is necessary to shake the conventionality of the public. He has, however, the head of a musician; but his eyes and gestures are those of a Superman, to quote Nietzsche, from whose teaching he must have imbibed his energy. From Nietzsche too he must have learned his lofty scorn of feeble sentimentalities and his desire that music should not go on for ever providing a more or less satisfactory illumination for our nights, but that it should shine like the sun. I can assure you that there is sunshine in the music of Strauss. Unquestionably the majority of the audience did not like sunshine of this kind, for quite famous musical enthusiasts showed unmistakable signs of impatience. But that did not prevent Strauss from being greeted with rapturous applause. I say again that it is not possible to withstand his irresistible domination.

XVI   Richard Wagner

The *Société des Grandes Auditions de France*[1] did not honour me with an invitation to listen to the recent performance of *Parsifal* at the *Nouveau-Théâtre* under the director, Alfred Cortot.[2] Alfred Cortot is the French conductor who has used to the best advantage the pantomime customary to German conductors. Like Nikisch[3]—who, however, is Hungarian —he has a lock of hair, and that lock is in the highest degree arresting owing to the quivers of passion which agitate it on the slightest provocation. Sometimes it droops sadly and wearily in the tender passages, interposing a complete screen between Cortot and the orchestra. Then again it rears itself proudly in

[1] The *Société des Grandes Auditions Musicales de la France* was founded about twenty-five years ago by the Countess Greffulhe. The moving spirit was Raoul Gunsbourg (see note 1, p. 61). Its activities were erratic and ceased to all intents and purposes about 1911.

[2] Alfred Denis Cortot, born Nyon, Switzerland, 1877; educated at the Paris Conservatoire, studied under Decambes, Rouquon and Diemer, winning the piano prize in 1896, and in that year made his debut at the Colonne concerts. He arranged and produced the first performance in Paris of *The Götterdämmerung* in 1902. From 1902 to 1911 he was director of the Chorus at Bayreuth. His first performance in England was at the Queen's Hall Orchestra Symphony Concert on February 14th, 1914.

[3] See Note p. 27.

the martial passages. At such moments Cortot advances on the orchestra and aims a threatening baton, like a banderillero when he wants to irritate the bull. The members of the orchestra are as cool as Icelanders: they have been there before. Cortot, like Weingartner, leans affectionately over the first violins, murmuring intimate secrets; he swoops round to the trombones, adjuring them with an eloquent gesture, that might be translated: "Now my lads! Put some go into it! Try to be supertrombones!" and the obedient trombones conscientiously do their best to swallow the brass tubes.

It is only fair to add that Cortot understands the innermost secrets of Wagner and is himself a perfect musician. He is young, his love of music is quite distinterested; and these are good reasons enough for not being too hard on him for gestures that are more decorative than useful.

To return to the *Société des Grandes Auditions,* did it intend to punish me for my Wagnerian iconoclasm by depriving me of *Parsifal?* Did it fear a subversive attitude or a bombshell? I do not know, but I should prefer to think that these private performances are designed for people whose nobility or position in high society entitles them to attend such little entertainments with a well-bred indifference to what is played. The unimpeachable distinction of the name on the programme frees them from the need of any other illumination and makes it possible to listen attentively to the latest scandal or to watch those pretty movements of the heads of women who are not listening to music. But let the *Société des Grandes Auditions* beware! They will turn Wagner's music into a fashionable at home. After all, that phase of Wagnerian art which originally imposed on his votaries costly pilgrimages and mysterious rites is irritating. I am well aware that this Religion of Art was one of Wagner's favourite ideas; and he was right, for such a formula is excellent for capturing and holding the imagination of an audience; but it has miscarried by becoming a kind of Religion of Luxury, excluding perforce many people who are richer in enthusiasm than in cash. The *Société des Grandes Auditions,* by carrying on these traditions of exclusiveness, seems to me doomed to end in that most detestable thing, the art of fashionable society. When Wagner was in a good humour he liked to maintain that he would never

be so well understood as in France. Was he referring to aristo-
cratic performances only? I do not think so. King Louis II of
Bavaria[1] was already annoying him enough with questions of
arbitrary etiquette; and Wagner's proud sensitiveness was too
acute to miss the fact that true fame comes solely from the masses
and not from a more or less gilded and exclusive public. It is
to be feared that these performances, directed avowedly at the
diffusion of Wagnerian art, may serve only to alienate the sympathy of the masses: a cunning trick to make it unpopular. I
do not mean that the performances will hasten a final eclipse;
for Wagner's art can never completely die. It will suffer that
inevitable decay, the cruel brand of time on all beautiful things;
yet noble ruins must remain, in the shadow of which our grand-
children will brood over the past splendour of this man who,
had he been a little more human, would have been altogether
great.

In *Parsifal,* the final effort of a genius which compels our
homage, Wagner tried to drive his music on a looser rein and let
it breathe more freely. We have no longer the distraught breath-
lessness that characterises Tristan's morbid passion or Isolde's
wild screams of frenzy; nor yet the grandiloquent commentary on
the inhumanity of Wotan. Nowhere in Wagner's music is a more
serene beauty attained than in the prelude to the third act of
Parsifal and in the entire Good Friday episode; although, it
must be admitted that Wagner's peculiar conception of human
nature is also shown in the attitude of certain characters in this
drama. Look at Amfortas, that melancholy Knight of the Grail,
who whines like a shop girl and whimpers like a baby. Good
heavens! A Knight of the Grail, a king's son, would plunge his
spear into his own body rather than parade a guilty wound in
doleful melodies for three acts! As for Kundry, that ancient
rose of hell, she has furnished much copy for Wagnerian literature; and I confess I have but little affection for such a sentimental draggle-tail. Klingsor is the finest character in *Parsifal:*
a quondam Knight of the Grail, sent packing from the Holy
Place because of his too pronounced views on chastity. His

---

[1] King Louis of Bavaria became Wagner's patron in 1864. It was
due to him that Wagner became a naturalised Bavarian, and for him
that Wagner wrote the *Huldigungsmarsch.*

bitter hatred is amazing; he knows the worth of men and scornfully weighs the strength of their vows of chastity in the balance. From this it is quite obvious that this crafty magician, this old gaol-bird, is not merely the only human character but the only moral character in this drama, in which the falsest moral and religious ideas are set forth, ideas of which the youthful Parsifal is the heroic and insipid champion.

Here in short is a Christian drama in which nobody is willing to sacrifice himself, though sacrifice is one of the highest of the Christian virtues! If Parsifal recovers his miraculous spear, it is thanks to old Kundry, the only creature actually sacrificed in the story: a victim twice over, once to the diabolical intrigues of Klingsor and again to the sacred spleen of a Knight of the Grail. The atmosphere is certainly religious, but why have the incidental children's voices such sinister harmonies? Think for a moment of the childlike candour that would have been conveyed if the spirit of Palestrina had been able to dictate its expression.

The above remarks only apply to the poet whom we are accustomed to admire in Wagner and have nothing to do with the musical beauty of the opera, which is supreme. It is incomparable and bewildering, splendid and strong. *Parsifal* is one of the loveliest monuments of sound ever raised to the serene glory of music.

XVII *Siegfried Wagner*

Siegfried Wagner[1] bears lightly the heavy burden of glory left him by his illustrious father. He does not seem even to be aware of it, such is the tranquil assurance of his precise, detached attitude. His likeness to his father is remarkable; but it is a copy which lacks the touch of genius of the original. In his youth apparently he was destined for architecture. We shall never know whether architecture lost very much when later he turned aside to music; nor is it certain that

---

1 Siegfried Wagner, born 1871, was the son of Richard Wagner and Cosima, Liszt's daughter, formerly wife of Hans von Bülow.

music gained very much either. All things considered, it is undoubtedly the part of a dutiful son to wish to carry on his father's tradition, but in such a case it is not as easy as taking over a haberdasher's shop. It is not a question of Siegfried's inability to grasp what was beyond him in his father's work, but the fact that he made the attempt implies an attitude of mind in which the most childish vanity is mingled with the desire to dedicate his work to the honour of a beloved memory. On the other hand it was difficult to escape the seductive atmosphere of Bayreuth without endeavouring to drain the magician's cup; unfortunately, however, only the dregs of the magic potion remain, nor do they smell of anything but vinegar. These ideas occurred to me as I listened to fragments of Siegfried Wagner's three-act musical comedy, *Duc Wildfang* [*Herzog Wildfang*]. It is decent music and nothing more; something like the task of a pupil who, had he studied under Richard Wagner, would not greatly have attracted the master's notice.

Siegfried Wagner, when giving the *Siegfried Idyll*—which, by the way, he conducts exceedingly well—would have perhaps been wise to listen to the gentle, persuasive voice of maternal affection which pervades this work. The Idyll would have urged him to pass through life freely and joyfully immune from the anxieties and disappointments of the pursuit of fame. It harped upon his name and endued it with a lasting radiance. Why has he sought new fields of fame which will always be equivocal and will leave him, when all is said and done, with only the title of the son of Richard Wagner, in my opinion his only enviable title?

The mind of another, however, is a dark forest in which we must step warily. Siegfried Wagner has no doubt better reasons than those by which I try to explain him. He seemed to me inferior as a conductor to those generally exported from Germany. Among others, Weingartner has more understanding, Nikisch is more decorative. Why too is he so finicking in his rendering of Beethoven's Symphony in A,[1] as to weaken it and make it even rather absurd?

---

[1] Beethoven's 7th Symphony in A major, op. 92.

XVIII *César Franck*

César Franck's *Béatitudes*[1] does not re-
quire any staging; it is pure music; and, moreover, it is con-
sistently beautiful music. César Franck was single minded. To
have found a beautiful harmony sufficed to make his day happy.
A rather closer examination of the verses of the *Béatitudes* reveals
such a collection of images and truisms as to daunt the most
resolute man alive. It required the sane and unruffled genius of
César Franck smilingly to grapple with it all like a kindly apostle
preaching the gospel and saying:

"Be not troubled—God will recognise his own."

Yet a strange impression is produced by the characteristic
melodiousness of César Franck interpreting verses which would
disgrace a penny whistle. Meanwhile, there has been much dis-
cussion of the genius of César Franck, but never a word about his
unique quality, simplicity. Unhappy and misunderstood as he
was, he still had the heart of a child, so fundamentally good
that he could, without a trace of bitterness, contemplate the
wickedness of mankind and the perversity of things.

It was thus that he wrote those too facilely dramatic choruses,
those persistently and wearisomely monotonous elaborations,
which seem sometimes to mar the beauty of the *Béatitudes*, with
that candour and confidence which enlist our admiration when
he is face to face with music, before which he kneels murmuring the most profoundly human prayer ever uttered by a mortal
soul. He never thinks evil or suspects boredom. There is none of
the trickery so flagrant when Wagner performs a sentimental
or orchestral pirouette by which he stimulates the attention of
an audience wearied sometimes by a too continuous breathing
of a rarefied atmosphere.

César Franck is always a worshipper of music, and you can
take it or leave it; no power on earth can induce him to interrupt a period which he considers just and necessary; however
long it is, it must be gone through. This is the hall-mark of an

1 César Franck, born Liége, 1822, died Paris, 1890; ranked as the
greatest of modern French teachers and was probably the greatest of
church organists and composers since Bach. Among his best-known works
are *Les Béatitudes* and his Symphony in D.

imagination so selfless as to check its very sobs unless it has first tested their genuineness.

In this César Franck is allied to the great masters for whom tones have an exact meaning within their own sphere; they use them with precision and without ever exacting from them more than is explicit in them. Here lies all the difference between the impure art of Wagner, with its peculiar beauty and seduction, and the art of Franck, which renders service to music without expecting any return. What he takes from life he restores to art with a modesty which is almost selfless. When Wagner takes from life he conquers it, places his foot on its neck and forces it to shriek the name of Wagner louder than the trumpets of Fame. I should have liked to have portrayed César Franck more precisely in order that each reader might have in his mind a clear picture of him. Amid all our preoccupations and distractions we ought to think of the great musicians; and still more, to make others think of them.

Good Friday seemed to me the right day on which to pay homage to one of the greatest of them; for the idea of sacrifice which calls for our homage on this sacred day is inherent also in his greatness.

XIX   Neglect

The dead are really sometimes too diffident and are willing to wait too long for the sad meed of posthumous fame.

To lift the veil from death tactful hands are needed. It usually happens however that the hands which exhume are clumsy and suspicious; they cast the poor funeral flowers into oblivion under the influence of a base and unavowed egoism. The blaze of glory that surrounds Bach really obscures Händel for us. His oratorios, more numerous than the sands of the sea, are unknown to us and, like the sands, contain more pebbles than pearls; it is however certain that they would repay patient and discriminating study.

Another master now quite forgotten is Alessandro Scarlatti,[1] the founder of the Neapolitan school, who composed a positively amazing number and variety of works. The statement seems incredible that Scarlatti, born in 1659, had written by 1715 more than 106 operas—not to mention all kinds of other musical compositions. Good heavens! How gifted the man must have been; and how could he find time to live? We know a *Passion According to St. John* by him, a little masterpiece of primitive grace, in which the choruses seem to be written in pale gold like the halos which set off so delicately the virgin faces seen in the frescoes of his period. This music is much less fatiguing to listen to than *The Rhinegold* and the hushed emotion exhaled from it is gently consoling. I cannot imagine how he found time to have a son and to make a distinguished harpsichord player of him. He is still appreciated to-day under the name of Domenico Scarlatti.[2]

There are many others, but do not be afraid: I do not propose to make a contribution to the history of music. I merely want to suggest that perhaps it is wrong always to play the same things, which might make quite decent people think that music was only born yesterday; whereas it has a past whose ashes are worth stirring, for within them lingers that unquenchable flame to which the present will always owe something of its radiance.

XX   *Grieg*

Grieg is the Scandinavian composer who was scarcely kind to France at the time of the Dreyfus Case. In a letter answering M. Colonne's[3] invitation to come and conduct his orchestra, Grieg declared vigorously that never again would

---

[1] Alessandro Scarlatti, born Sicily, 1658 or 1659, died 1725.

[2] Domenico Scarlatti, born Naples, 1684, died there 1757.

[3] Edouard Judas Colonne, born Bordeaux, 1838, died Paris, 1910; ranked with the best of modern conductors. In 1873 he founded the *Concerts nationaux*, which quickly became known as the Concerts Colonne. They are given on Saturday and Sunday afternoons; the audiences consist chiefly of students and business people. Colonne specialised in the works of Berlioz and Beethoven.

he set foot in a country which understood freedom so ill. Consequently France had to get on without Grieg. But, apparently, Grieg could not get on without France, because to-day he is quite willing to ignore his quarrel and the frontiers, in order to conduct a French orchestra which was once the object of his Scandinavian contempt. Besides, the Dreyfus Case is nearly dead and Grieg is almost sixty, an age when passions ought naturally to be appeased and give place to the calm wisdom of the sage who contemplates the course of events as a spectator who has weighed and appraised their irresistible march. Even though one is a Scandinavian one is human. It is hard to deny oneself the welcome which Paris extends so charmingly to foreigners, many of whom do not equal Grieg in their appeal to the artistic ear.

At first I thought that I could only give colour impressions of Grieg's music! To begin with, the number of Norwegians who usually haunt the Colonne Concerts was tripled; we had never before been privileged to see so much red hair, or such extravagant hats—for the fashions in Christiania seem to me rather behind the times. Then the concert opened with a double turn: the performance of an overture called *Autumn* and the ejection of a crowd of Grieg's admirers, who, at the bidding of a police-constable, a slave to duty rather than to music, were sent to cool their enthusiasm on the banks of the Seine. Was a counter-demonstration feared?

It is not for me to say, but Grieg was in fact for a time the object of the most unappreciative comments; nor could I listen to the music just then, for I was busily engaged in coming to terms with several stern and splendid policemen.

At last I saw Grieg. From in front he looks like a genial photographer; from behind his way of doing his hair makes him look like the plants called sunflowers, dear to parrots and the gardens that decorate small country stations. Despite his age, he is lean and vivacious and conducts the orchestra with care and vigour, stressing all the lights and shades and apportioning the expression with unflagging attention.

It is a pity that Grieg's visit to Paris has taught us nothing new about his art; but he is an exquisite musician when he interprets the folk music of his country, although far from equalling Balakirev[1] and Rimsky-Korsakov[2] in the use they make of Russian folk music. Apart from this, he is no more than a clever musician, more concerned with effects than with genuine art. Apparently his real inspiration was a young man of his own age, Richard Nordruck,[3] a born genius who would have been a great musician had he not died in his twenty-fourth year. His death was a twofold misfortune, since it robbed Norway of a great man and Grieg of a friendly influence which would certainly have prevented him from going astray.

For the rest, Grieg sets out, like Solness in *The Master Builder,* one of the late Ibsen plays, "to build homes for human beings. Cosy, happy homes. . . ."

I found no trace of this beautiful ideal in the music Grieg gave to us yesterday. Perhaps because as yet we know nothing of his later works. These may be Ibsen's "cosy homes!" Anyhow, Grieg did not give us the pleasure of entering them. The triumphant welcome he received yesterday may compensate him for his trouble in coming to France. Let our most heartfelt wish be that in the future he may deem us worthy of finding ourselves, if not "cosy," at least "happy" through his music.

XXI   Vincent d'Indy

L'Étranger[4] is what dogmatic people call an example of pure and lofty art, but in my humble opinion it is more than that.

It is the working out of formulas which are admittedly pure and lofty, but which have the coldness, blueness, delicacy and

1 Mily Alexeivich Balakirev, born Nijny-Novgorod, 1836; died St. Petersburg, 1910; founded the New Russian School.

2 Nicholas Andreievich Rimsky-Korsakov, born Tikhuin, Novgorod, 1844, died 1908.

3 Richard Nordruck (Nordraak), born Christiania, 1842; died 1866; composed incidental music to Björnson's "Mary Stuart"; assisted Grieg in collecting and editing Norwegian folk music.

4 Paul Marie Théodore Vincent d'Indy, born Paris, 1851; a pupil of César Franck; among his best-known works are the operas *L'Étranger* and *Fervaal.*

hardness of steel. Beautiful music is there, but it is, as it were, cloaked; and the mastery is so amazing that one hardly ventures to feel anything so incongruous as an emotion.

Say what you will, Wagner's influence on Vincent d'Indy was never really profound; Wagner was a strolling player on the heroic plane and could never be linked to so strict an artist as d'Indy. If *Fervaal* owes something to the influence of the Wagnerian tradition, it is protected from it by its conscientious scorn of the grandiloquent hysteria which ravages the Wagnerian heroes.

I am well aware that Vincent d'Indy will be reproached with having freed himself and with having lost his love for the hearth and home of the *leit-motif*—the delight of old Wagnerians whose steps are guided by special signposts.

Why did he not free himself entirely from the craving to explain everything, to emphasize everything, which sometimes burdens the finest scenes in *L'Étranger*?

What is the object of so much music for an excise officer, an incidental character with whose anxiety to oppose the overflowing humanity of "the Stranger" I sympathise, but who I could wish were more of a good fellow, more truly one of those ordinary human beings who think of nothing but their own wretched skins?

The dramatic action of *L'Étranger* is not, in spite of its simplicity, a mere chronicle of events. The action takes place in a small fishing village by the sea. A man has recently come to live in this village; he is called "the Stranger" for want of a better name; his personality is repellent and he neither makes friends with nor speaks to anyone; his cap is adorned with an emerald which naturally wins him the reputation of a sorcerer. He tries to be helpful and kindly, giving his share of fish to those who have caught nothing, and endeavours to set free an unfortunate man who is being dragged to prison; but the authorities have no love for wearers of symbols—nor have the fishermen.

In two simple phrases Vincent d'Indy has conveyed the character of the Stranger with great clarity. He is a Christian hero, in direct lineal descent from the martyrs who performed on earth tasks of charity imposed on them by God. The Stranger is, then, the faithful servant whom the Master decides to tempt through the love of a woman. He weakens and death alone can redeem him.

No modern music has expressed profound piety and Christian charity so well. Indeed, it is d'Indy's deep conviction which makes these two phrases so entirely successful; they light up the profound meaning of the drama better than any other sort of symphonic commentary.

A young girl, Vita, is attracted by the mystery and the brooding melancholy of this man; she has a passion for the sea to which she always confides her griefs and hopes. She is, however, betrothed to André, the handsome excise officer, who in a domestic scene proves himself a self-satisfied egoist. He is an official who is incapable of understanding that a girl can dream of anything but a handsome excise officer.

In a scene where Vita and the Stranger meet, the plot reaches its climax. Vita confesses her love. Since the arrival of the Stranger she has ceased to confide in the sea. Deeply moved, the Stranger inadvertently reveals his sad secret:

"Farewell, Vita. All happiness be thine. Tomorrow I go hence. For I love thee, I love thee, yes, I love thee passionately and well thou knowest it."

Vita is young and she is betrothed to another. The Stranger, by uttering words of love, has lost the purity of heart which was his strength; for moral solitude is necessary to the mission of redemption to which he is vowed. To devote himself to all forbids his devoting himself to one. It is no fun to work miracles every day. After all, the Stranger is old; and this purely human weakness is rather welcome in so superhuman a character.

He has for one moment forgotten his mission and is henceforth debarred from his task of charity. He gives Vita the now useless emerald and bids her an eternal farewell. Vita, weeping bitterly, throws the accursed emerald, the cause of her unhappiness, into the restless sea whence mysterious voices arise. The sea closes over the gem with a wild joy in every wave at having recaptured the talisman which had been wont to calm its unwilling waters. A storm arises; a vessel is in distress. As might be expected the honest fishermen of the first act do not dare to go to its aid.

André, the handsome excise officer, takes advantage of the general confusion to come and show Vita his new stripe and to offer her a beautiful silver bracelet. He goes too far in his egoism and Vita, by her silence, shows him how unwelcome his attentions are. He goes away unabashed. The Stranger arrives recalled by the danger, demands a small boat, and is about to put off alone since no one is willing to share the peril. Vita darts forward and, breaking into one of the most beautiful melodies ever inspired by love, joins the Stranger. They embark and vanish amid the fury of the waves which they no longer have the power to calm. An old sailor follows their struggle with his eyes. Suddenly the rope holding them to the shore breaks. The old sailor takes off his cap and solemnly pronounces the words of the *De Profundis*. These two souls have found peace in death, the only refuge for their hopeless love.

Let anyone who will look for mysterious symbolism in this plot. I prefer to see a simple human story which d'Indy has only expressed symbolically to make more absolute the eternal divorce of Beauty from the mob.

Without pausing to consider questions of technique, I want to do honour to the spirit of goodness hovering over this work, to the effort that avoids all complication and especially to the unshrinking boldness of Vincent d'Indy in his lofty aim. If I complained just now of too much music, it was because I thought that here and there it marred the perfect balance which distinguishes so many pages of *L'Étranger* with unforgettable beauty. This work is an admirable lesson to those who believe in the crude, imported style which consists in crushing music under cartloads of realism.

The Théâtre de la Monnaie and its directors are much to be congratulated on producing *L'Étranger* with an artistic care worthy of the highest praise. Possibly the staging might have received more careful attention. We ought however to be grateful for an enterprise which, even in these days, remains courageous.

I have nothing but praise for Sylvain Dupuis[1] and his or-

---

[1] Sylvain Dupuis, the Belgian composer, born 1856; conducted the performances of the *Théâtre de la Monnaie* in Brussels and the *Concerts populaires* in the same city from 1900 onwards.

chestra for that sympathetic understanding which is so precious to a musician. M. Albert and Mlle. Friché contributed to the triumph with which the name of the composer was received. Indeed, everyone displayed a touching enthusiasm and I see no reason why we should not congratulate the city of Brussels.

XXII Richter

It is not for me to say precisely in what the superiority of Anglo-Saxons consists, but, amongst other things, they have Covent Garden. This theatre possesses the peculiar characteristic of making music seem to be at home there. More attention is given to perfect acoustics than to sumptuous decorations and the orchestra is numerous and well disciplined. Besides all this, André Messager[1] assumes the artistic responsibilities with the perfect and unerring taste which everyone expects from him. You see how astonishing all this is, for they actually think that a musician can manage an opera house successfully! They really must be mad—or else they are systematic! In any case I shall institute no comparisons; they would establish too completely the poverty of our own methods, and our national pride might suffer. Only let us avoid false notes in blowing the trumpet of Fame on behalf of the glory of our own Opera; or, at all events, let us use a mute.

Recently I attended the performances of *The Rhinegold* and *The Valkyrie*. It seems to me impossible to achieve greater perfection. Although the scenery and certain lighting effects might be open to criticism, the artistic care shown throughout compels our admiration.

Richter[2] conducted the first performance of *The Ring* at Bayreuth in 1876. At that time his hair and beard were red-

---

1 André Charles Prosper Messager, born Montluçon, 1853; the composer of the light operas, *Véronique, Les P'tites Michus*, etc.; was made "Artistic Director" at Covent Garden for several seasons.

2 Hans Richter, born Raab, Hungary, 1843, died Bayreuth, 1916; the foremost of Wagnerian conductors; presided over the London Philharmonic Concerts in 1879 and over the Hallé concerts in Manchester from 1900.

gold; now his hair has gone, but behind his gold spectacles his eyes still flash magnificently. They are the eyes of a prophet; and he is in fact a prophet which he only ceases to be, at least as far as the Wagnerian cult is concerned, through Mme. Cosima Wagner's[1] decision to replace him by her estimable but mediocre son, Siegfried Wagner.

It was a sound arrangement from the point of view of domestic economy, but deplorable for the fame of Wagner. Such a man as Wagner needs men like Richter, Levy[2] or Mottl[3] —they are part of the splendid adventure which, at a given stage, brought Wagner into touch with a king—not to mention Liszt, whom he conscientiously plagiarised and who met him with nothing but a kindly smile of acquiescence.

There was something miraculous in Wagner, and his impunity as a despot almost excused his imperturbable vanity.

If Richter looks like a prophet, when he conducts the orchestra he is Almighty God: and you may be sure that God Himself would have asked Richter for some hints before embarking on such an adventure.

While his right hand, armed with a small unpretentious baton, secures the precision of the rhythm, his left hand, multiplied a hundredfold, directs the performance of each individual. This left hand is "undulating and diverse," its suppleness is unbelievable! Then, when it seems that there is really no possibility of attaining a greater wealth of sound, up go his two arms, and the orchestra leaps through the music with so furious an onset as to sweep the most stubborn indifference before it like a straw. Yet all this pantomime is unobtrusive and never distracts the attention unpleasantly or comes between the music and the audience.

I tried in vain to meet this marvellous man. He is a sage who shrinks in wild alarm from interviews. I caught sight of him for a moment as he rehearsed Fafner, the unfortunate dragon on whom that heroic little simpleton, Siegfried, was just about to test the virtue of his sword. It is easy to understand my emo-

---

1 See Note p. 49.

2 Hermann Levi (Levy), born Giessen, 1839, died Munich, 1900; was conductor at Carlsruhe and Munich; conducted the first performance of *Parsifal* at Bayreuth.

3 See Note 3, p. 21.

tion as I watched the conscientious old man bent over the piano while he performed the duties of a mere producer. Could I interrupt so excellent a man on the futile pretext of extracting confidences from him? Would it not be as outrageous as a presumptuous offer suddenly to extract one of his teeth?

You may be sure that the German theatres had been ransacked to discover singers worthy of such a performance. I wish I could mention them all. For to-day, I will refer only to Van Dyck, who interpreted the ironic fantasy of Loki in *The Rhinegold,* and the impassioned poetry of Siegmund in *The Valkyrie.* M. Lieban in his astonishing performance of the sly and obsequious dwarf, Mime, sang marvellously. These two men are great artists.

Mlle. Zimmermann almost made us forget Mme. Caron, who used to invest the rôle of Sieglinde with such poignant charm. As for the three Rhine maidens, I only wish you could have heard them.

An English audience listens with almost rapt attention. If any boredom is felt there is no sign of it. On the other hand the theatre is plunged in darkness throughout the acts, so that it is possible to sleep in perfect safety. Following the strict Wagnerian tradition, there was no applause until the end of each act, when Richter went off contentedly, oblivious of it and impatient, maybe, to find recuperation in a glass of beer.

XXIII Berlioz

Berlioz never had any luck. He suffered from the inadequacy of the orchestras and the intellects of his time. To-day, however, the inventive genius of M. Gunsbourg,[1] supported by the *Société des Grandes Auditions Musicales de France,* has undertaken to revive and to augment Berlioz's posthumous glory by adapting *The Damnation of Faust* to the stage.

[1] Raoul Gunsbourg, born at Bukarest, 1859; is a literary man, a composer and Director of the Opera at Monte Carlo. He organised a series of performances of *La Damnation de Faust* adapted for the stage. See note 1 on *La Société des Grandes Auditions Musicales de la France* on p. 46.

Without condemning the policy of such an adaptation we may at least urge the undeniable fact that, since Berlioz died without leaving any precise views on its suitability, it is æsthetically debatable. Besides this, to step into a dead man's shoes without a specific invitation seems to me a deliberate flouting of the respect which we usually show to the dead. But here again M. Gunsbourg's unwavering confidence in his own genius gives him a natural right to treat Berlioz as a brother, and to carry out instructions which have probably come to him from beyond the grave.

In doing this M. Gunsbourg carries on the unfortunate tradition which requires masterpieces to breed a teeming horde of commentators, adapters and manipulators, whose representatives spring into existence without any further definite function than that of befogging with pompous words and epithets the said unhappy masterpieces.

Berlioz, alas, is not the only victim! There is the smile of the famous *Gioconda*, which a strange perversity has labelled for all time mysterious. There is Beethoven's *Choral Symphony* which has been subjected to such transcendental interpretations, that even such a powerful and straightforward work as this has become a universal nightmare. There is the whole work of Wagner, which needed all its solidity to withstand the industrious enthusiasm of its editors.

Such practices result in a kind of special literature and even in a recognised profession in which success is certain provided the beaten track is never left, since its members being engaged in criticising others are bound to be immune from the danger of mutual criticism. In some respects it is a laudable profession; in others it seems to have a certain futility, though a greater or less degree of cleverness may win fame for its members.

So far, Berlioz had escaped any such intrusion; only Jullien,[1] in an admirably documented book, had piously recorded the calvary of his fame and Fantin-Latour had interpreted his music in lithographic dreams. Incidentally, the work of Berlioz, through his pre-occupation with colour and incident, became at once a subject for artists; one might even say without irony that

[1] Adolphe Jullien, the author of *Hector Berlioz, sa vie et ses œuvres*, illustrated with fourteen original lithogravures by Fantin-Latour, Paris, 1888.

Berlioz has always been the favourite musician of those who do not know much about music. Other musicians are alarmed at the liberties he takes with harmony—they even call them blunders— and his "Go-to-the-devil!" style. Are these the reasons which make his influence on modern music negligible and leave his own, in a way, unique? In France, with the exception of Gustave Charpentier,[1] I can hardly find a trace of his influence, and even there only in a superficial sense, since Charpentier's art is un-doubtedly individual as far as concerns anything that is funda-mental in his music.

This brings me to the fact that Berlioz was never, properly speaking, a stage-musician. Despite the real beauties of *Les Troyens*, a lyrical tragedy in two parts, faulty proportions make its performance difficult and produce an almost monotonous, not to say wearisome, effect. For the rest, Berlioz has nothing new to offer in this work. He echoes Gluck, whom he passionately ad-mired, and Meyerbeer, whom he religiously hated. We must not seek Berlioz here. We must seek him in his pure symphonic music or in his *Enfance du Christ*, which is perhaps his master-piece; nor must we forget the *Symphonie Fantastique* and the music of his *Romeo and Juliet*.

But M. Gunsbourg was on the watch and said: "My dear Berlioz, you know nothing about it! If you have never succeeded on the stage, it is because, unfortunately, I was not at hand to help you with my experience. Now you are dead, and we can put everything to rights. Listen! You composed a dramatic legend, *The Damnation of Faust*. It is not bad, but it is not alive! And what interest can you expect people to take in your *Marche Hongroise* if they do not see soldiers exercising at the back of the stage? As for your *Ballet des Sylphes*, it is most charming music. But you will never make me believe that a mere symphony orchestra can ever take the place of an attractive ballet dancer! Your *Course à l'Abîme* is terrifying, my dear fellow! But you wait and see; I will make it poignant and ghastly. I will turn aside the course of rivers in order to make natural waterfalls; I will make a rain of real blood supplied by the slaughter-houses; the horses of Faust and Mephistopheles shall trample upon real

[1] See Note 1, p. 40.

corpses. Fortunately, too, you won't be able to interfere! You were so eccentric when you were alive that your presence could only spoil the whole thing."

So saying, M. Gunsbourg set to work and adapted frantically. As he made his way through *Faust* he was even more convinced that this "confounded Berlioz" knew nothing whatever about it. "Too much music," he grumbled, and "what facility!" but "it is disconnected, I must have recitatives. It is a pity that he is really dead, but it can't be helped! We must get along without him." And M. Gunsbourg got along without him; he added recitatives and altered the order of the scenes. Everything, or nearly everything, gave him an excuse for ballets and supers, resulting in a performance in which the tricks of the pantomime were combined with the attractions of the *Folies-Bergère*.

At Monte Carlo it might have succeeded. People do not go there just to listen to beautiful music, which has about as much importance for them as a fine afternoon. The delightful adventurers who adorn that resort are not very particular, and the charming cosmopolitan young ladies only regard music as an unobtrusive and useful accompaniment to their smiles.

Something better was essential for Paris; so the *Société des Grandes Auditions*, for whose well-known eclecticism no sacrifice is too great, intervened. In this case, it sems to me, they sacrificed everything, even the most elementary good taste. Their desire to give France lessons in the best music has, I fear, carried them beyond all bounds; but the fashionable set, owing to a lack of interest, may be more easily deceived than others. Besides that, there were admirable singers such as M. Renaud, perhaps the only artist who, by his tact and good taste, could make the Mephistopheles, conceived by the fancy of M. Gunsbourg, tolerable. M. Alvarez and Mme. Calvé are too celebrated not to be perfect, even in *Faust*. But, good Heavens! what marionettes they had to be!

Finally, there are two beings who would have been amazed at the performance. In the first place Faust, though he did meet his old friend M. Colonne, would have been astonished at finding himself filling the passages in which he had been accustomed to keep still with a pantomime which he would be at a loss to understand. In the second place the Spirit of Music would have recoiled from the consciousness of often being *de trop* or even utterly unnecessary. She is so little at home on the stage, poor thing, that she blushes at the sound of her own voice and at the awkward figure she cuts in the staging imposed on her by M. Gunsbourg.

For the future, M. Gunsbourg may sleep in peace. His bust will face that of Berlioz in the gardens at Monte Carlo; he will be much more at home there, and Berlioz will certainly have no reason to complain of his proximity.

XXIV Gounod

Many unbiassed people—that is to say, people who are not musicians—wonder why the Opera persists in giving Gounod's *Faust*. There are several reasons, the chief being that Gounod's art represents a phase of French æsthetic development. Whether we like it or not, such things are not forgotten.

As to *Faust*, eminent writers on music have reproached Gounod with travestying Goethe's conception; but the same eminent writers never think of noticing that Wagner may have misrepresented the character of Tannhäuser, who, in the legend, is not at all the repentant little scapegrace Wagner makes him out to be, nor did his staff, scorched by the memory of Venus, ever flower again. Gounod is a Frenchman and may therefore be forgiven; but in the case of Wagner, since he and Tannhäuser were both Germans, it is inexcusable.

We love so many things in France that we do not really love music. Yet there are very clever people who, by dint of hearing all kinds of music every day, profess to be musicians. But they never write music—they encourage others. That is generally how a school is started. You must not mention Gounod to them; they would look scornfully down on you from among their Olympians, whose most delightful quality is that they are interchangeable. Gounod did not belong to any school. The masses are in much the same position. Their reply to the countless artistic invitations is a return to the familiar, which is not always in the best taste. They may oscillate blindly between *Père la Victoire*[1] and *The Valkyrie*, but there it is. The people who so oddly constitute the elect may loudly trumpet famous or respectable names, but the fashion changes as with hats. It is no use; educators may waste their breath, but the great vague heart of the people refuses to be caught; art continues to blow where it listeth, and the Opera persists in giving *Faust*.

We must make the best of it, however, and admit that art is of absolutely no use to the masses; it does not even express the mind of the *élite* who are often more stupid than the masses. It is the expression of beauty in full flower which blossoms at its appointed time at the bidding of a mysterious destiny. One can no more compel the masses to love beauty than one can decently ask them to stand on their heads. In passing, it is noteworthy that the spontaneous effect of Berlioz on the masses is practically invariable.

If Gounod's influence is questionable, Wagner's is obvious, though, since it never extends beyond the specialists, it is in fact incomplete. We are bound to admit that nothing was ever more dreary than the neo-Wagnerian school in which the French genius has lost its way among the sham Wotans in Hessian boots and the Tristans in velvet jackets.

Although Gounod may lack the sweeping harmony that we could wish for him, he deserves our praise for having evaded the domination of the genius of Wagner, whose peculiarly German ideal was not clearly realised in his attempt at a fusion of the arts. It has become hardly more than a formula for the advancement of literature.

Gounod, with all his faults, is needed. To begin with, he is cultured; he knows Palestrina and draws upon Bach. His respect for tradition is discriminating enough for him not to be swept away by Gluck, another rather indeterminate foreign influence. It is rather Mozart for whom he asks the affection of young people, which is a proof of great disinterestedness, for he never drew inspiration from him. His relations with Mendelssohn were

---

[1] This popular patriotic French aid was written in the late 'eighties during the presidency of Sadi Carnot. Its theme was the anticipated reorganisation of the French army by Carnot as it had been reorganised in 1793 by the previous Carnot, called *l'Organisateur de la Victoire*.

more obvious, since it is to him that he owes his method, so convenient when the flow of inspiration fails, of developing the melody step by step. Generally speaking, Mendelssohn's influence was perhaps more direct than that of Schumann. Bizet[1] he ignores, and that is a very good thing. Bizet, unfortunately, died too soon and, although he left a masterpiece, the development of French music was not affected. French music is still in the position of a pretty widow who, having no one by her side strong enough to direct her, falls, to her cost, into alien arms. It is undeniable that certain unions are necessary in art, but we should at least use some discretion; to choose the loudest shouter is not necessarily to choose the finest man. These unions are too often merely self-interested and little more than a means of reviving a waning fame. Like cautious marriages, they turn out badly. Let us magnanimously accept such art as is imported into France, only let us not be blinded or fall into ecstasies over penny whistles. Let us make up our minds that this valuation will not be reciprocated; on the contrary, our good nature induces that stern and discourteous attitude in foreigners, of which we can hardly complain since we have challenged it. To conclude these notes which are too brief for the ideas with which they deal and which are sometimes depreciatory of Gounod, let us, without being over dogmatic, take the opportunity of rendering our homage to him. Let it be stated once again that a name lives in the memory of men for various though not necessarily weighty reasons. One of the best means of achieving this is to stir the emotions of the majority of one's contemporaries. Of that no one will deny Gounod made generous use.

XXV   An Open Letter to the Chevalier W. Gluck

Sir,—Shall I write to you or shall I summon your spirit? My letter would probably not reach you; and

---

1 Georges Alexandre César Léopold Bizet, born Paris, 1838, died Bougival, near Paris, 1875; among his best-known works are *Carmen* and *l'Arlésienne*.

it is doubtful whether you would consent to leave the abode of the blessed to come and talk to me about the fate of an art in which you excelled to such a degree that you might reasonably expect to have your name omitted from interminable discussions on the subject. I shall, therefore, employ both and endow you with an imaginary life which allows me a certain freedom. You will, I hope, pardon me for not admiring your work; I shall not on that account forget the respect due to so famous a man.

You were in fact a court musician. Royal hands turned the pages of your manuscripts and you enjoyed the approbation of painted smiles. There was a great to-do about you and a man called Piccini[1] who composed over sixty operas. You were the victim of the universal law that quantity shall take the place of quality, and that Italians shall at all times glut the music market. The said Piccini has been so completely forgotten that he has had to take the name of Puccini[2] in order to get himself performed at the *Opéra Comique*. However, discussions between cultured priests and dogmatic encyclopædists can hardly have affected you; both sides spoke of music with an incompetence that you would find as common to-day. It is true that you showed your independence by conducting the first performance of *Iphigenia in Aulis* with your nightcap instead of your wig on your head, but it was even more important for you to please your king and queen. You must accept the fact that such illustrious associations have lent to your music an almost uniformly pompous bearing. When your characters fall in love, they do so with majestic dignity; even suffering makes a preliminary obeisance. Is it more elegant to please King Louis XIV than to please society under the Third Republic? That is a question which your status as a dead man prevents me from deciding in the affirmative.

Your art was essentially in the grand ceremonious style. Common people only participated at a distance. They were used to seeing others pass by who were more fortunate and more com-

---

[1] Niccola Piccini, born Paris, 1779, died Paris, 1850; rivalled Gluck in popular fame as a composer of opera. The musicians of France were divided into two hostile camps, but the Gluck party carried the day. Piccini's influence on opera is negligible.

[2] Giacomo Puccini, born Lucca, 1858; among his best-known works are *Manon Lescaut, La Bohème, La Tosca, Madame Butterfly.*

fortable than themselves. You represented to them, as it were, a wall behind which something was happening.

We have changed all that, my dear Chevalier, for we have a social sense and we endeavour to reach the heart of the masses. We are not succeeding any better and it does not make us any prouder of ourselves! You have no idea how hard it is for us to found a People's Opera.

In spite of the "luxurious" aspect of your art, it has had considerable influence on French music. You can be traced in Spontini,[1] Lesueur,[2] Méhul[3] and others; you embody the Wagnerian formulas in embryo, which is intolerable; you will see why in a moment. Between ourselves, your words and music harmonise badly; in any case, you make the French language one of accentuation, whereas it is a language of inflection. I know you are a German. Rameau, who helped to form your genius, gives examples of fine and vigorous declamation which ought to have been more useful to you—I say nothing about the musician in Rameau, because I do not wish to be offensive to you. It is owing to you that the action of the drama now dominates the music. Is that really desirable? All things considered, I prefer Mozart to you; the splendid fellow entirely ignores you and thinks of nothing but music. To attain that domination you took Greek subjects, which accounts for the solemn nonsense that is talked about the alleged connection between your music and Greek art.

Rameau was infinitely more Greek than you. Do not fly into a passion—I shall soon be leaving you. Moreover, Rameau was lyrical, which suited us from all points of view; we had only to remain lyrical and had no need to wait for a century of music to revive that quality in us.

Through knowing you French music enjoyed the somewhat

[1] Gasparo Luigi Pacifico Spontini, born Majolati, near Jesi, 1774, died 1851; enjoyed fame as a musician during his lifetime, but failed to create anything of permanent value.

[2] Jean François Lesueur, born Drucat-Plessiel, near Abbéville, 1760, died Paris, 1837; his best-known works are the operas *Télémaque, Paul et Virginie* and *La Caverne*.

[3] Etienne Nicholas Henri Méhul, born Givel, Ardennes, 1763, died Paris, 1817; his *Joseph* and other popular operas were written under the influence of Gluck.

unlooked-for blessing of falling into the arms of Wagner; I like to think that, but for you, not only would this not have happened, but that French music would not have asked its way so often of people who were only too ready to lead it astray.

In conclusion, you have benefited by the many false interpretations given to the word "classic"; but to have invented a purring accompaniment to drama, sacrificing any attempt at music, does not entitle you to be called a "classic." Rameau has more serious claims to such a title.

I am sorry, because of Mme. Caron's performance, that you are dead. She presented your Iphigenia as a type of purity infinitely more Greek than any you ever conceived. There was not an attitude or a gesture which was not of supreme beauty.

All the deep emotion you failed to embody in this character was discovered by Mme. Caron. Her every step was music. Could you have seen how she went to sit by the sacred tree before the sacrifice in the third act, you would have wept, so poignant a grief was there in that simple movement.

And when, at the end of the opera, you unite the tender Iphigenia and the faithful Pylades in the bonds of Hymen, Mme. Caron's face was so radiantly transfigured that one forgot the commonplace banality of this climax in admiration of her violet eyes; a colour, as you know, especially dear to all who dream vaguely of Greek beauty.

In this woman your music is idealised; it is no longer labelled with a period; for, by a gift, which makes us believe in the survival of the ancient gods, hers is the soul of tragedy which raises the dark veil from the past and calls to life again those dead cities where the worship of Beauty was harmoniously wedded to the worship of Art.

M. Cossira would have delighted you with the charm of his voice, and M. Dufrane by the convincing way in which he roared the fury of Orestes. I did not much care for the Scythian interlude in the first act, which suggests at once the Russian moujik and the antics of a party of cabmen. Your warlike interludes, allow me to say, are most difficult to perform; for neither the music, nor the rhythm gives any very precise guide. You may rest assured that everywhere else M. Carré has found the proper setting.

And with this, my dear Chevalier,
I have the honour to remain,
Your very humble servant,
CLAUDE DEBUSSY.

Sketch of a New Esthetic

of Music

Ferruccio Busoni

What seek you? Say! And what do you expect?—
I know not what; the Unknown I would have!
What's known to me, is endless; I would go
Beyond the end: The last word still is wanting.
                    ["*Der mächtige Zauberer.*"]

1

Loosely joined together as regards literary form, the following notes are, in reality, the outcome of convictions long held and slowly matured.

In them a problem of the first magnitude is formulated with apparent simplicity, without giving the key to its final solution; for the problem cannot be solved for generations—if at all.

But it involves an innumerable series of lesser problems, which I present to the consideration of those whom they may concern. For it is a long time since any one has devoted himself to earnest musical research.

It is true, that admirable works of genius arise in every period, and I have always taken my stand in the front rank of those who joyfully acclaimed the passing standard-bearers; and still it seems to me that of all these beautiful paths leading so far afield—none lead *upward*.

The spirit of an art-work, the measure of emotion, of humanity, that is in it—these remain unchanged in value through changing years; the form which these three assumed, the manner of their expression, and the flavor of the epoch which gave them birth, are transient, and age rapidly.

Spirit and emotion retain their essence, in the art-work as in man himself; we admire technical achievements, yet they are outstripped, or cloy the taste and are discarded.

Its ephemeral qualities give a work the stamp of "modernity;" its unchangeable essence hinders it from becoming "obsolete." Among both "modern" and "old" works we find good and bad, genuine and spurious. There is nothing properly modern—only things which have come into being earlier or later; longer in bloom, or sooner withered. The Modern and the Old have always been.

Art-forms are the more lasting, the more closely they adhere to the nature of their individual species of art, the purer they keep their essential means and ends.

Sculpture relinquishes the expression of the human pupil, and effects of color; painting degenerates, when it forsakes the flat surface in depiction and takes on complexity in theatrical decoration or panoramic portrayal.

Architecture has its fundamental form, growth from below upward, prescribed by static necessity; window and roof necessarily provide the intermediate and finishing configuration; these are eternal and inviolable requirements of the art.

Poetry commands the abstract thought, which it clothes in words. More independent than the others, it reaches the furthest bounds.

But all arts, resources and forms ever aim at the one end, namely, the imitation of nature and the interpretation of human feelings.

Architecture, sculpture, poetry and painting are old and mature arts; their conceptions are established and their objects assured; they have found the way through uncounted centuries, and, like the planets, describe their regular orbits.[1]

Music, compared with them, is a child that has learned to walk, but must still be led. It is a virgin art, without experience in life and suffering.

It is all unconscious as yet of what garb is becoming, of its own advantages, its unawakened capacities. And again, it is a child-marvel that is already able to dispense much of beauty, that has already brought joy to many, and whose gifts are commonly held to have attained full maturity.

Music as an art, our so-called occidental music, is hardly four hundred years old; its state is one of development, perhaps the very first stage of a development beyond present conception,

[1] None the less, in these arts, taste and individuality can and will unceasingly find refreshment and rejuvenation.

and we—we talk of "classics" and "hallowed traditions"! And we have talked of them for a long time![1]

We have formulated rules, stated principles, laid down laws;—we apply laws made for maturity to a child. that knows nothing of responsibility!

Young as it is, this child, we already recognize that it possesses one radiant attribute which signalizes it beyond all its elder sisters. And the lawgivers will not see this marvelous attribute, lest their laws should be thrown to the winds. This child —it *floats on air!* It touches not the earth with its feet. It knows no law of gravitation. It is wellnigh incorporeal. Its material is transparent. It is sonorous air. It is almost Nature herself. It is— free.

But freedom is something that mankind have never wholly comprehended, never realized to the full. They can neither recognize nor acknowledge it.

They disavow the mission of this child; they hang weights upon it. This buoyant creature must walk decently, like anybody else. It may scarcely be allowed to leap—when it were its joy to follow the line of the rainbow, and to break sunbeams with the clouds.

Music was born free; and to win freedom is its destiny. It will become the most complete of all reflexes of Nature by reason of its untrammeled immateriality. Even the poetic word ranks lower in point of incorporealness. It can gather together and disperse, can be motionless repose or wildest tempestuosity; it has the extremest heights perceptible to man—what other art has these?—and its emotion seizes the human heart with that intensity which is independent of the "idea."

It realizes a temperament, *without* describing it, with the mobility of the soul, with the swiftness of consecutive moments; and this, where painter or sculptor can represent only one side

---

1 Tradition is a plaster mask taken from life, which, in the course of many years, and after passing through the hands of innumerable artisans, leaves its resemblance to the original largely a matter of imagination.

or one moment, and the poet tardily *communicates* a temperament and its manifestations by words.

Therefore, representation and description are not the nature of music; herewith we declare the invalidity of program-music, and arrive at the question: What are the aims of music?

2

Absolute Music! What the lawgivers mean by this, is perhaps remotest of all from the Absolute in music. "Absolute music" is a form-play without poetic program, in which the form is intended to have the leading part. But Form, in itself, is the opposite pole of absolute music, on which was bestowed the divine prerogative of buoyancy, of freedom from the limitations of matter. In a picture, the illustration of a sunset ends with the frame; the limitless natural phenomenon is enclosed in quadrilateral bounds; the cloud-form chosen for depiction remains unchanging for ever. Music can grow brighter or darker, shift hither or yon, and finally fade away like the sunset glow itself; and instinct leads the creative musician to employ the tones that press the same key within the human breast, and awaken the same response, as the processes in Nature.

Per contra, "absolute music" is something very sober, which reminds one of music-desks in orderly rows, of the relation of Tonic to Dominant, of Developments and Codas.

Methinks I hear the second violin struggling, a fourth below, to emulate the more dexterous first, and contending in needless contest merely to arrive at the starting-point. This sort of music ought rather to be called the "architectonic," or "symmetric," or "sectional," and derives from the circumstance that certain composers poured *their* spirit and *their* emotion into just this mould as lying nearest them or their time. Our lawgivers have identified the spirit and emotion, the individuality of these composers and their time, with "symmetric" music, and finally, being powerless to recreate either the spirit, or the emotion, or the time, have retained the Form as a symbol, and made it into a fetish, a religion. The composers sought and found this form as the aptest vehicle for communicating *their* ideas; their souls took flight— and the lawgivers discover and cherish the garments Euphorion left behind on earth.

A lucky find! 'Twas now or never;
The flame is gone, it's true—however,
  No need to pity mankind now.
Enough is left for many a poet's tiring,
  Or to breed envy high and low;
And though I have no talents here for hiring,
  I'll hire the robe out, anyhow.

Is it not singular, to demand of a composer originality in all things, and to forbid it as regards form? No wonder that, once he becomes original, he is accused of "formlessness." Mozart! the seeker and the finder, the great man with the childlike heart—it is he we marvel at, to whom we are devoted; but not his Tonic and Dominant, his Developments and Codas.

Such lust of liberation filled Beethoven, the romantic revolutionary, that he ascended one short step on the way leading music back to its loftier self:—a short step in the great task, a wide step in his own path. He did not quite reach absolute music, but in certain moments he divined it, as in the introduction to the fugue of the Sonata for Hammerclavier. Indeed, all composers have drawn nearest the true nature of music in preparatory and intermediary passages (preludes and transitions), where they felt at liberty to disregard symmetrical proportions, and unconsciously drew free breath. Even a Schumann (of so much lower stature) is seized, in such passages, by some feeling of the boundlessness of this pan-art (recall the transition to the last movement of the D-minor Symphony); and the same may be asserted of Brahms in the introduction to the Finale of his First Symphony.

But, the moment they cross the threshold of the *Principal Subject,* their attitude becomes stiff and conventional, like that of a man entering some bureau of high officialdom.

Next to Beethoven, Bach bears closest affinity to "infinite music."[1] His Organ Fantasias (but not the Fugues) have indubitably a strong dash of what might be overwritten "Man and

---

1 "Die Ur-Musik," is the author's happy phrase. But as this music *never has been,* our English terms like "primitive," "original," etc., would involve a *non sequitur* which is avoided, at least, by "infinite." [Translator's Note.]

Nature."[1] In him it appears most ingenuous because he had no reverence for his predecessors (although he esteemed and made use of them), and because the still novel acquisition of equal temperament opened a vista of—for the time being—endless new possibilities.

Therefore, Bach and Beethoven[2] are to be conceived as a *beginning*, and not as unsurpassable finalities. In spirit and emotion they will probably remain unexcelled; and this, again, confirms the remark at the beginning of these lines: That spirit and emotion remain unchanged in value through changing years, and that he who mounts to their uttermost heights will always tower above the crowd.

What still remains to be surpassed, is their form of expression and their freedom. Wagner, a Germanic Titan, who touched our earthly horizon in orchestral tone-effect, who intensified the form of expression, but fashioned it into a *system* (music-drama, declamation, leading-motive), is on this account incapable of further intensification. His category begins and ends with himself; first, because he carried it to the highest perfection and finish; secondly, because his self-imposed task was of such a nature, that it could be achieved by one man alone.[3] The paths opened by Beethoven can be followed to their end only through generations. They—like all things in creation—may form only a circle; but a circle of such dimensions, that the portion visible to us seems like a straight line. Wagner's circle we can view in its entirety—a circle within the great circle.

3

The name of Wagner leads to program-music. This has been set up as a contrast to so-called "absolute"

[1] In the recitatives of his Passions we hear "human speech"; *not* "correct declamation."

[2] As characteristic traits of Beethoven's individuality I would mention the poetic fire, the strong human feeling (whence springs his revolutionary temper), and a portent of modern nervousness. These traits are certainly opposed to those of a "classic." Moreover, Beethoven is no "master," as the term applies to Mozart or the later Wagner, just because his art foreshadows a greater, as yet incomplete. (Compare the section next-following.)

[3] "Together with the problem, it gives us the solution," as I once said of Mozart.

music, and these concepts have become so petrified that even persons of intelligence hold one or the other dogma, without recognition for a third possibility beyond and above the other two. In reality, program-music is precisely as one-sided and limited as that which is called absolute. In place of architectonic and symmetric formulas, instead of the relation of Tonic to Dominant, it has bound itself in the stays of a connecting poetic —sometimes even philosophic—program.

Every motive—so it seems to me—contains, like a seed, its life-germ within itself. From the different plant-seeds grow different families of plants, dissimilar in form, foliage, blossom, fruit, growth and color.[1]

Even each individual plant belonging to one and the same species assumes, in size, form and strength, a growth peculiar to itself. And so, in each motive, there lies the embryo of its fully developed form; each one must unfold itself differently, yet each obediently follows the law of eternal harmony. *This form is imperishable, though each be unlike every other.*

The motive in a composition with program bears within itself the same natural necessity; but it must, even in its earliest phase of development, renounce *its own proper mode of growth* to mould—or, rather, twist—itself to fit the needs of the program. Thus turned aside, at the outset, from the path traced by nature, it finally arrives at a wholly unexpected climax, whither it has been led, not by its own organization, but by the way laid down in the program, or the action, or the philosophical idea.

And how primitive must this art remain! True, there are unequivocal descriptive effects of tone-painting (from these the entire principle took its rise), but these means of expression are few and trivial, covering but a very small section of musical art. Begin with the most self-evident of all, the debasement of Tone to Noise in imitating the sounds of Nature—the rolling of thunder, the roar of forests, the cries of animals; then those somewhat less evident, symbolic—imitations of visual impressions, like the lightning-flash, springing movement, the flight of birds; again,

1 ". . . Beethoven, dont les esquisses *thématiques ou élémentaires* sont innombrables, mais qui, sitôt les thèmes trouvés, semble par cela même en avoir établi tout le développement . . ." [Vincent d' Indy, in "César Franck."]

those intelligible only through the mediation of the reflective
brain, such as the trumpet-call as a warlike symbol, the shawm
to betoken ruralism, march-rhythm to signify measured strides,
the chorale as vehicle for religious feeling. Add to the above the
characterization of nationalities—national instruments and airs—
and we have a complete inventory of the arsenal of program-
music. Movement and repose, minor and major, high and low, in
their customary significance, round out the list.—These are auxil-
iaries, of which good use can be made upon a broad canvas, but
which, taken by themselves, are no more to be called music than
wax figures may pass for monuments.

And, after all, what can the presentation of a little happening upon this earth, the report concerning an annoying neighbor
—no matter whether in the next room or in an adjoining quarter
of the globe—have in common with that music which pervades
the universe?

To music, indeed, it is given to set in vibration our human
moods: Dread (*Leporello*), oppression of soul, invigoration,
lassitude (Beethoven's last Quartets), decision (*Wotan*), hesita-
tion, despondency, encouragement, harshness, tenderness, excitement, tranquillization, the feeling of surprise or expectancy, and
still others; likewise the inner echo of external occurrences which
is bound up in these moods of the soul. But not the moving
cause itself of these spiritual affections;—not the joy over an
avoided danger, not the danger itself, or the kind of danger
which caused the dread; an emotional state, yes, but not the
psychic species of this emotion, such as envy, or jealousy; and it
is equally futile to attempt the expression, through music, of
moral characteristics (vanity, cleverness), or abstract ideas like
truth and justice. Is it possible to imagine how a poor, but contented man could be represented by music? The contentment,
the soul-state, can be interpreted by music; but where does the
poverty appear, or the important ethic problem stated in the
words "poor, but contented"? This is due to the fact that "poor"
connotes a phase of terrestrial and social conditions not to be
found in the eternal harmony. And Music is a part of the vibra-
ting universe.

I may be allowed to subjoin a few subsidiary reflections:— The greater part of modern theatre music suffers from the mistake of seeking to repeat the scenes passing on the stage, instead of fulfilling its own proper mission of interpreting the soul-states of the persons represented. When the scene presents the illusion of a thunderstorm, this is exhaustively apprehended by the eye. Nevertheless, nearly all composers strive to depict the storm in tones—which is not only a needless and feebler repetition, but likewise a failure to perform their true function. The person on the stage is either psychically influenced by the thunderstorm, or his mood, being absorbed in a train of thought of stronger influence, remains unaffected. The storm is visible and audible without aid from music; it is the invisible and inaudible, the spiritual processes of the personages portrayed, which music should render intelligible.

Again, there are "obvious" psychic conditions on the stage, whereof music need take no account. Suppose a theatrical situation in which a convivial company is passing at night and disappears from view, while in the foreground a silent, envenomed duel is in progress. Here the music, by means of continuing song, should keep in mind the jovial company now lost to sight; the acts and feelings of the pair in the foreground may be understood without further commentary, and the music—dramatically speaking—ought not to participate in their action and break the tragic silence.

Measurably justified, in my opinion, is the plan of the old opera, which concentrated and musically rounded out the passions aroused by a moving dramatic scene in a piece of set form (the aria). *Word* and stage-play conveyed the dramatic progress of the action, followed more or less meagrely by musical recitative; arrived at the point of rest, music resumed the reins. This is less extrinsic than some would now have us believe. On the other hand, it was the ossified form of the "aria" itself which led to inveracity of expression and decadence.

4

The audible presentation, the "perform-
ance," of music, its *emotional interpretation*, derives from those
free heights whence descended the Art itself. Where the art is
threatened by earthliness, it is the part of interpretation to raise
it and reëndow it with its primordial essence.

Notation, the writing out of compositions, is primarily an
ingenious expedient for catching an inspiration, with the purpose of exploiting it later. But notation is to improvisation as
the portrait to the living model. It is for the interpreter to
resolve the rigidity of the signs into the primitive emotion.

But the lawgivers require the interpreter to reproduce the
rigidity of the signs; they consider his reproduction the nearer
to perfection, the more closely it clings to the signs.—

What the composer's inspiration *necessarily* loses[1] through
notation, his interpreter should restore by his own.

To the lawgivers, the signs themselves are the most important matter, and are continually growing in their estimation; the
new art of music is derived from the old signs—*and these now
stand for musical art itself.*

If the lawgivers had their way, any given composition would
always be reproduced in precisely the same tempo, whensoever,

---

[1] How strongly notation influences style in music, and fetters imagination, how "form" grew up out of it and from form arose "conventionalism"
in expression, is shown very convincingly and avenges itself in tragic wise
in E. T. A. Hoffmann, who occurs to me here as a typical example.

This remarkable man's mental conceptions, lost in visionary moods
and revelling in transcendentalism, as his writings set forth in oft inimitable
fashion, must naturally—so one would infer—have found in the dreamlike
and transcendental art of tones a language and mode of expression peculiarly
congenial.

The veil of mysticism, the secret harmonies of Nature, the thrill of
the supernatural, the twilight vagueness of the borderland of dreams, everything, in fact, which he so effectively limned with the precision of *words*
—all this, one would suppose, he could have interpreted to fullest effect by
the aid of music. And yet, comparing Hoffmann's best musical work with
the weakest of his literary productions, you will discover to your sorrow
how a conventional system of measures, periods and keys—whereto the
hackneyed opera-style of the time adds its share—could turn a poet into
a Philistine. But that his fancy cherished another ideal of music, we learn
from many, and frequently admirable, observations of Hoffmann the
littérateur.

by whomsoever, and under whatsoever conditions it might be performed.

But, it *is* not possible; the buoyant, expansive nature of the divine child rebels—it demands the opposite. Each day begins differently from the preceding, yet always with the flush of dawn. —Great artists play their own works differently at each repetition, remodel them on the spur of the moment, accelerate and retard, in a way which they could not indicate by signs—and always according to the given conditions of that "eternal harmony."

And then the lawgiver chafes, and refers the creator to his own handwriting. As matters stand to-day, the lawgiver has the best of the argument.

"Notation" ("writing down") brings up the subject of Transcription, nowadays a term much misunderstood, almost discreditable. The frequent antagonism which I have excited with "transcriptions," and the opposition to which an ofttimes irrational criticism has provoked me, caused me to seek a clear understanding of this point. My final conclusion concerning it is this: Every notation is, in itself, the transcription of an abstract idea. The instant the pen seizes it, the idea loses its original form. The very intention to write down the idea, compels a choice of measure and key. The form, and the musical agency, which the composer must decide upon, still more closely define the way and the limits.

It is much the same as with man himself. Born naked, and as yet without definite aspirations, he decides, or at a given moment is made to decide, upon a career. From the moment of decision, although much that is original and imperishable in the idea or the man may live on, either is depressed to the type of a class. The musical idea becomes a sonata or a concerto; the man, a soldier or a priest. That is an Arrangement of the original. From this first transcription to a second the step is comparatively short and unimportant. And yet it is only the second, in general, of which any notice is taken; overlooking the fact, that a transcription does not destroy the archetype, which is, therefore, not lost through transcription.

Again, the performance of a work is also a transcription, and still, whatever liberties it may take, it can never annihilate the original.

For the musical art-work exists, before its tones resound and after they die away, *complete and intact*. It exists both within and outside of time, and through its nature we can obtain a definite conception of the otherwise intangible notion of the Ideality of Time.

For the rest, most of Beethoven's piano compositions sound like transcriptions of orchestral works; most of Schumann's orchestral compositions, like arrangements from pieces for the piano—and they are so, in a way.

Strangely enough, the Variation-Form is highly esteemed by the Worshippers of the Letter. That is singular; for the variation-form—when built up on a borrowed theme—produces a *whole series of "arrangements"* which, besides, are least respectful when most ingenious.

So the arrangement is *not* good, because it *varies* the original; and the variation *is* good, although it *"arranges"* the original.

5

The term "musikalisch" (musical) is used by the Germans in a sense foreign to that in which any other language employs it.[1] It is a conception belonging to the Germans, and not to culture in general; the expression is incorrect and untranslatable. "Musical" is derived from *music*, like "poetical" from *poetry*, or "physical" from *physic (s)*. When I say, "Schubert was one of the most musical among men," it is the same as if I should say, "Helmholtz was one of the most physical among men." That is musical, which *sounds* in rhythms and intervals. A cupboard can be "musical," if "music-works" be enclosed in it.[2] In a comparative sense, "musical" may have the fur-

---

[1] The author probably had in mind the languages of southern Europe; the word is employed in English, and in the tongues of the Scandinavian group, with precisely the same meaning as in German. [Translator's Note.]

[2] The only kind of people one might properly call *musical*, are the singers; for they themselves can sound. Similarly, a clown who by some trick produces tones when he is touched, might be called a *pseudo-musical* person.

ther signification of "euphonious."—"My verses are too musical to bear setting to music," a noted poet once remarked to me.

> "Spirits moving musically
> To a lute's well-tuned law,"

writes Edgar Allan Poe. Lastly, one may speak quite correctly of "musical laughter," because it *sounds* like music.

Taking the signification in which the term is applied and almost exclusively employed in German, a musical person is one who manifests an inclination for music by a nice discrimination and sensitiveness with regard to the *technical aspects* of the art. By "technics" I mean rhythm, harmony, intonation, part-leading, and the treatment of themes. The more subtleties he is capable of hearing or reproducing in these, the more "musical" he is held to be.

In view of the great importance attached to these elements of the art, this "musical" temperament has naturally become of the highest consequence. And so an artist who plays with perfect technical finish should be deemed the most musical player. But as we mean by "technics" only the mechanical mastery of the instrument, the terms "technical" and "musical" have been turned into opposites.

The matter has been carried so far as to call a composition itself "musical,"[1] or even to assert of a great composer like Berlioz that he was not sufficiently musical.[2] "Unmusical" conveys the strongest reproach; branded thus, its object becomes an outlaw.[3]

In a country like Italy, where all participate in the delights of music, this differentiation becomes superfluous, and the term corresponding is not found in the language. In France, where a living sense of music does not permeate the people, there are musicians and non-musicians; of the rest, some "are very fond of music," and others "do not care for it." Only in Germany is it made a point of honor to be "musical," that is to say, not merely to love music, but more especially to understand it as regards

---

1 "But these pieces are so musical," a violinist once remarked to me of a four-hand worklet which I had characterized as trivial.

2 "My dog is *very* musical," I have heard said in all seriousness. Should the dog take precedence of Berlioz?

3 Such has been my own fate.

its technical means of expression, and to obey their rules.

A thousand hands support the buoyant child and solicitously attend its footsteps, that it may not soar aloft where there might be risk of a serious fall. But it is still so young, and is eternal; the day of its freedom will come.—When it shall cease to be "musical."

6

The creator should take over no traditional law in blind belief, which would make him view his own creative endeavor, from the outset, as an exception contrasting with that law. For his individual case he should seek out and formulate a fitting individual law, which, after the first complete realization, he should annul, that he himself may not be drawn into repetitions when his next work shall be in the making.

The function of the creative artist consists in making laws, not in following laws ready made. He who follows such laws, ceases to be a creator.

Creative power may be the more readily recognized, the more it shakes itself loose from tradition. But an intentional avoidance of the rules cannot masquerade as creative power, and still less engender it.

The true creator strives, in reality, after *perfection* only. And through bringing this into harmony with *his own* individuality, a new law arises without premeditation.

So narrow has our tonal range become, so stereotyped its form of expression, that nowadays there is not one familiar motive that cannot be fitted with some other familiar motive so that the two may be played simultaneously. Not to lose my way in trifling,[1] I shall refrain from giving examples.

[1] With a friend I once indulged in such trifling in order to ascertain how many commonly known compositions were written according to the scheme of the second theme in the Adagio of the Ninth Symphony. In a few moments we had collected some fifteen analogues of the most different kinds, among them specimens of the lowest type of art. And Beethoven himself:—Is the theme of the Finale in the "Fifth" any other than the one wherewith the "Second" introduces its Allegro?—or than the principal theme of the Third Piano Concerto, only in minor?

That which, within our present-day music, most nearly approaches the essential nature of the art, is the Rest and the Hold (Pause). Consummate players, improvisers, know how to employ these instruments of expression in loftier and ampler measure. The tense silence between two movements—*in itself music,* in this environment—leaves wider scope for divination than the more determinate, but therefore less elastic, sound.

What we now call our Tonal System is nothing more than a set of "signs"; an ingenious device to grasp somewhat of that eternal harmony; a meagre pocket-edition of that encyclopedic work; artificial light instead of the sun.—Have you ever noticed how people gaze open-mouthed at the brilliant illumination of a hall? They never do so at the millionfold brighter sunshine of noonday.—

And so, in music, the signs have assumed greater consequence than that which they ought to stand for, and can only suggest.

How important, indeed, are "Third," "Fifth," and "Octave"! How strictly we divide "consonances" from "dissonances" —*in a sphere where no dissonances can possibly exist!*

We have divided the octave into twelve equidistant degrees, because we had to manage somehow, and have constructed our instruments in such a way that we can never get in above or below or between them. Keyboard instruments, in particular, have so thoroughly schooled our ears that we are no longer capable of hearing anything else—incapable of hearing except through this impure medium. Yet Nature created an *infinite gradation—infinite!* who still knows it nowadays?[1]

---

[1] "The equal temperament of 12 degrees, which was discussed theoretically as early as about 1500, but not established as a principle until shortly before 1700 (by Andreas Werkmeister), divides the octave into twelve equal portions (semitones, hence 'twelve-semitone system') through which mean values are obtained; no interval is perfectly pure, but all are fairly serviceable." (Riemann, "Musik-Lexikon.") Thus, through Andreas Werkmeister, this master-workman in art, we have gained the "twelve-semitone" system with intervals which are all impure, but fairly serviceable. But what is "pure," and what "impure"? We hear a piano "gone out of tune," and whose intervals may thus have become "pure, but unserviceable," and it sounds *impure* to us. The diplomatic "Twelve-semitone system" is an invention mothered by necessity; yet none the less do we sedulously guard its imperfections.

And within this duodecimal octave we have marked out a series of fixed intervals, seven in number, and founded thereon our entire art of music. What do I say—*one* series? Two such series, one for each leg: The Major and Minor Scales. When we start this series of intervals on some other degree of our semitonic ladder, we obtain a *new key*, and a "foreign" one, at that! How violently contracted a system arose from this initial confusion,[1] may be read in the law-books; we will not repeat it here.

We teach four-and-twenty keys, twelve times the two Series of Seven; but, in point of fact, we have at our command only two, the major key and the minor key. *The rest are merely transpositions.* By means of the several transpositions we are supposed to get different shades of harmony; but this is an illusion. In England, under the reign of the high "concert pitch," the most familiar works may be played a semitone higher than they are written, without changing their effect. Singers transpose an aria to suit their convenience, leaving untransposed what precedes and follows. Songwriters not infrequently publish their own compositions in three different pitches; in all three editions the pieces are precisely alike.

When a well-known face looks out of a window, it matters not whether it gazes down from the first story or the third.

Were it feasible to elevate or depress a landscape, far as eye can reach, by several hundred yards, the pictorial impression would neither gain nor lose by it.

Upon the two Series of Seven, the major key and the minor key, the whole art of music has been established; one limitation brings on the other.

To each of these a definite character has been attributed; we have learned and have taught that they should be heard as contrasts, and they have gradually acquired the significance of symbols:—Major and Minor—Maggiore e Minore—Contentment and Discontent—Joy and Sorrow—Light and Shade. The harmonic symbols have fenced in the expression of music, from Bach to Wagner, and yet further on until to-day and the day after to-morrow. *Minor* is employed with the same intention, and

1 It is termed "The Science of Harmony."

has the same effect upon us now, as two hundred years ago. Nowadays it is no longer possible to "compose" a funeral march, for it already exists, once for all. Even the least informed non-professional knows what to expect when a funeral march—whichever you please—is to be played. Even such an one can anticipate the difference between a symphony in major and one in minor. We are tyrannized by Major and Minor—by the bifurcated garment.

Strange, that one should feel major and minor as opposites. They both present the same face, now more joyous, now more serious; and a mere touch of the brush suffices to turn the one into the other. The passage from either to the other is easy and imperceptible; when it occurs frequently and swiftly, the two begin to shimmer and coalesce indistinguishably.—But when we recognize that major and minor form one Whole with a double meaning, and that the "four-and-twenty keys" are simply an elevenfold transposition of the original twain, we arrive unconstrainedly at a perception of the UNITY *of our system of keys* [tonality]. The conceptions of "related" and "foreign" keys vanish, and with them the entire intricate theory of degrees and relations. *We possess one single key.* But it is of most meagre sort.

"Unity of the key-system."
—"I suppose you mean that 'key' and 'key-system' are the sunbeam and its diffraction into colors?"
No; that I can not mean. For our whole system of tone, key, and tonality, taken in its entirety, is only a part of a fraction of one diffracted ray from that Sun, "Music," in the empyrean of the "eternal harmony."

However deeply rooted the attachment to the habitual, and inertia, may be in the ways and nature of humankind, in equal measure are energy, and opposition to the existing order, characteristic of all that has life. Nature has her wiles, and persuades man, obstinately opposed though he be to progress and change; Nature progresses continually and changes unremittingly, but with so even and unnoticeable movement that men perceive only quiescence. Only on looking backward from a distance do they note with astonishment that they have been deceived.

The Reformer of any given period excites irritation for the reason that his changes find men unprepared, and, above all, because these changes are appreciable. The Reformer, in comparison with Nature, is undiplomatic; and, as a wholly logical consequence, his changes do not win general acceptance until Time, with subtle, imperceptible advance, has bridged over the leap of the self-assured leader. Yet we find cases in which the reformer marched abreast of the times, while the rest fell behind. And then they have to be forced and lashed to take the leap across the passage they have missed. I believe that the major-and-minor key with its transpositional relations, our "twelve-semitone system," exhibits such a case of falling behind.

That some few have already felt how the intervals of the Series of Seven might be differently arranged (graduated) is manifested in isolated passages by Liszt, and recently by Debussy and his following, and even by Richard Strauss. Strong impulse, longing, gifted instinct, all speak from these strains. Yet it does not appear to me that a conscious and orderly conception of this intensified means of expression had been formed by these composers.

I have made an attempt to exhaust the possibilities of the arrangement of degrees within the seven-tone scale; and succeeded, by raising and lowering the intervals, in establishing *one hundred and thirteen different scales*. These 113 scales (within the octave $C-C$) comprise the greater part of our familiar twenty-four keys, and, furthermore, a series of new keys of peculiar character. But with these the mine is not exhausted, for we are at liberty to *transpose* each one of these 113, besides the blending of two such keys in harmony and melody.

There is a significant difference between the sound of the scale c-d♭-e♭-f♭-g♭-a♭-b♭-c when c is taken as tonic, and the scale of d♭ minor. By giving it the customary C-major triad as a fundamental harmony, a novel harmonic sensation is obtained. But now listen to this same scale supported alternately by the A-minor, E♭-major, and C-major triads, and you cannot avoid a feeling of delightful surprise at the strangely unfamiliar euphony.

But how would a lawgiver classify the tone-series *c-db-eb-fb-g-a-b-c, c-db-eb-f-gb-a-b-c, c-d-eb-fb-gb-a-b-c, c-db-e-f-gb-a-bb-c?* — or these, forsooth: *c-d-eb-fb-g-a♯-b-c, c-d-eb-fb-g♯-a-b-c, c-db-eb-f♯-g♯-a-bb-c?*

One cannot estimate at a glance what wealth of melodic and harmonic expression would thus be opened up to the hearing; but a great many novel possibilities may be accepted as certain, and are perceptible at a glance.

With this presentation, the unity of all keys may be considered as finally pronounced and justified. A kaleidoscopic blending and interchanging of twelve semitones within the three-mirror tube of Taste, Emotion, and Intention—the essential feature of the harmony of to-day.

The harmony of *to-day,* and not for long; for all signs presage a revolution, and a next step toward that "eternal harmony." Let us once again call to mind, that in this latter the gradation of the octave is *infinite,* and let us strive to draw a little nearer to infinitude. The tripartite tone (third of a tone) has for some time been demanding admittance, and we have left the call unheeded. Whoever has experimented, like myself (in a modest way), with this interval, and introduced (either with voice or with violin) two equidistant intermediate tones between the extremes of a whole tone, schooling his ear and his precision of attack, will not have failed to discern that tripartite tones are wholly independent intervals with a pronounced character, and not to be confounded with ill-tuned semitones. They form a refinement in chromatics based, as at present appears, on the whole-tone scale. Were we to adopt them without further preparation, we should have to give up the semi-tones and lose our "minor third" and "perfect fifth;" and this loss would be felt more keenly than the relative gain of a system of eighteen one-third tones.

But there is no apparent reason for giving up the semitones for the sake of this new system. By retaining, for each whole tone, a semitone, we obtain a second series of whole tones lying a semitone higher than the original series. Then, by dividing this second series of whole tones into third-tones, each third-tone in the lower series will be matched by a semitone in the higher series.

Thus we have really arrived at a system of whole tones divided into sixths of a tone; and we may be sure that even sixth-tones will sometime be adopted into musical speech. But the tonal system above sketched must first of all train the hearing to thirds of a tone, without giving up the semitones.

To summarize: We may set up either two series of third-tones, with an interval of a semitone between the series; or, the usual semitonic series *thrice repeated* at the interval of one-third of a tone.

Merely for the sake of distinction, let us call the first tone *C*, and the next third-tones *C♯*, and *D♭*; the first semitone (small) c, and its following thirds c♯ and d♭; the result is fully explained by the table below:

A preliminary expedient for notation might be, to draw six lines for the staff, using the lines for the whole tones and the spaces for the semitones:

then indicating the third-tones by sharps and flats:

The question of notation seems to me subordinate. On the other hand, the question is important and imperious, how and on what these tones are to be produced. Fortunately, while busied with this essay, I received from America direct and authentic intelligence which solves the problem in a simple manner. I refer to an invention by Dr. Thaddeus Cahill.[1] He has constructed a comprehensive apparatus which makes it possible to transform an electric current into a fixed and mathematically exact number of vibrations. As pitch depends on the number of vibrations, and the apparatus may be "set" on any number desired, the infinite gradation of the octave may be accomplished by merely moving a lever corresponding to the pointer of a quadrant.

Only a long and careful series of experiments, and a continued training of the ear, can render this unfamiliar material approachable and plastic for the coming generation, and for Art.

And what a vista of fair hopes and dreamlike fancies is thus opened for them both! Who has not dreamt that he could float on air? and firmly believed his dream to be reality?—Let us take thought, how music may be restored to its primitive, natural essence; let us free it from architectonic, acoustic and esthetic dogmas; let it be pure invention and sentiment, in harmonies, in forms, in tone-colors (for invention and sentiment are not the prerogative of melody alone); let it follow the line of the rainbow and vie with the clouds in breaking sunbeams; *let Music be naught else than Nature mirrored by and reflected from the human breast;* for it is sounding air and floats above and beyond the air; within Man himself as universally and absolutely as in Creation entire; for it can gather together and disperse without losing in intensity.

7

In his book "Beyond the Good and the Bad" (*Jenseits von Gut und Böse*) Nietzsche says: "With regard to German music I consider precaution necessary in various ways.

1 "New Music for an Old World." Dr. Thaddeus Cahill's Dynamophone, an extraordinary electrical invention for producing scientifically perfect music. Article in McClure's Magazine for July, 1906, by Ray Stannard Baker. Readers interested in the details of this invention are referred to the above-mentioned magazine article.

Assuming that a person loves the South (as I love it) as a great training-school for health of soul and sense in their highest potency, as an uncontrollable flood and glamour of sunshine spreading over a race of independent and self-reliant beings;—well, such an one will learn to be more or less on his guard against German music, because while spoiling his taste anew, it undermines his health.

"Such a Southlander (not by descent, but by belief) must, should he dream of the future of music, likewise dream of a redemption of music from the North, while in his ears there rings the prelude to a deeper, mightier, perchance a more evil and more mysterious music, a super-German music, which does not fade, wither and die away in view of the blue, sensuous sea and the splendor of Mediterranean skies, as all German music does;—a super-European music, that asserts itself even amid the tawny sunsets of the desert, whose soul is allied with the palm-tree, and can consort and prowl with great, beautiful, lonely beasts of prey.

"I could imagine a music whose rarest charm should consist in its complete divorce from the Good and the Bad;—only that its surface might be ruffled, as it were, by a longing as of a sailor for home, by variable golden shadows and tender frailties:—an Art which should see fleeing toward it, from afar off, the hues of a perishing moral world become wellnigh incomprehensible, and which should be hospitable and profound enough to harbor such belated fugitives."

And Tolstoi transmutes a landscape-impression into a musical impression when he writes, in "Lucerne": "Neither on the lake, nor on the mountains, nor in the skies, a single straight line, a single unmixed color, a single point of repose;—everywhere movement, irregularity, caprice, variety, an incessant interplay of shades and lines, and in it all the reposefulness, softness, harmony and inevitableness of Beauty."

Will this music ever be attained?

"Not all reach Nirvana; but he who, gifted from the beginning, learns everything that one ought to learn, experiences all that one should experience, renounces what one should renounce, develops what one should develop, realizes what one should realize—he shall reach Nirvana."[1] (Kern, *Geschichte des Buddhismus in Indien.*)

If Nirvana be the realm "beyond the Good and the Bad," *one* way leading thither is here pointed out. A way to the very portal. To the bars that divide Man from Eternity—or that open to admit that which was temporal. Beyond that portal sounds *music.* Not the strains of "musical art."[2]—It may be, that we must leave Earth to find that music. But only to the pilgrim who has succeeded on the way in freeing himself from earthly shackles, shall the bars open.

Addenda

8

Feeling—like honesty—is a moral point of honor, an attribute of whose possession no one will permit denial, which claims a place in life and art alike. But while, in life, a want of feeling may be forgiven to the possessor of a more brilliant attribute, such as bravery or impartial justice, in art feeling is held to be the highest moral qualification.

In music, however, feeling requires two consorts, taste and style. Now, in life, one encounters real taste as seldom as deep and true feeling; as for style, it is a province of art. What remains, is a species of pseudo-emotion which must be characterized as lachrymose hysteria or turgidity. And, above all, people insist upon having it plainly paraded before their eyes! It must be underscored, so that everybody shall stop, look, and listen. The audience sees it, greatly magnified, thrown on the screen, so that it dances before the vision in vague, importunate vastness; it is cried on the streets, to summon them that dwell re-

---

1 As if anticipating my thoughts, M. Vincent d'Indy has just written me: ". . . laissant de côté les contingences et les petitesses de la vie pour regarder constamment vers un idéal qu'on ne pourra jamais atteindre, mais dont il est permis de se rapprocher."

2 I think I have read, somewhere, that Liszt confined his Dante Symphony to the two movements, *Inferno* and *Purgatorio,* "because our tone-speech is inadequate to express the felicities of Paradise."

mote from art; it is gilded, to make the destitute stare in amaze.

For in life, too, the *expressions* of feeling, by mien and words, are oftenest employed; rarer, and more genuine, is that feeling which acts without talk; and most precious is the feeling which hides itself.

"Feeling" is generally understood to mean tenderness, pathos, and extravagance, of expression. But how much more does the marvelous flower "Emotion" enfold! Restraint and forbearance, renunciation, power, activity, patience, magnanimity, joyousness, and that all-controlling intelligence wherein feeling actually takes its rise.

It is not otherwise in Art, which holds the mirror up to Life; and still more outspokenly in Music, which repeats the emotions of Life—though for this, as I have said, taste and style must be added; Style, which distinguishes Art from Life.

What the amateur and the mediocre artist attempt to express, is feeling in little, in detail, for a short stretch.

Feeling on a grand scale is mistaken by the amateur, the semi-artist, the public (and the critics too, unhappily!), for a want of emotion, because they all are unable to hear the longer reaches as parts of a yet more extended whole. Feeling, therefore, is likewise economy.

Hence, I distinguish feeling as Taste, as Style, as Economy. Each a whole in itself, and each one-third of the Whole. Within and over them rules a subjective trinity: Temperament, Intelligence, and the instinct of Equipoise.

These six carry on a dance of such subtility in the choice of partners and intertwining of figures, in the bearing and the being borne, in advancing and curtseying, in motion and repose, that no loftier height of artistry is conceivable.

When the chords of the two triads are in perfect tune, Fantasy may—nay, must—associate with Feeling; supported by the Six, she will not degenerate, and out of this combination of all the elements arises Individuality. The individuality catches, like a lens, the light-impressions, reflects them, according to its nature, as a negative, and the hearer perceives the true picture.

In so far as taste participates in feeling, the latter—like all else—alters its forms of expression with the period. That is, one aspect or another of feeling will be favored at one time or another, onesidedly cultivated, especially developed. Thus, with and after Wagner, voluptuous sensuality came to the fore; the form of *intensification of passion* is still unsurmounted by contemporary composers. On every tranquil beginning followed a swift upward surge. Wagner, in this point insatiable, but not inexhaustible, turned from sheer necessity to the expedient, after reaching a climax, of starting afresh softly, to soar to a sudden new intensification.

Modern French writers exhibit a revulsion; their feeling is a reflective chastity, or perhaps rather a restrained sensualism; the upstriving mountain-paths of Wagner are succeeded by monotonous plains of twilight uniformity.

Thus "style" forms itself out of feeling, when led by taste.

The "Apostles of the Ninth Symphony" have devised the notion of "depth" in music. It is still current at face-value, especially in Germanic lands.

There is a depth of feeling, and a depth of thought; the latter is literary, and can have no application to tones. Depth of feeling, by contrast, is psychical, and thoroughly germane to the nature of music. The Apostles of the Ninth Symphony have a peculiar and not quite clearly defined estimate of "depth" in music. *Depth* becomes *breadth,* and the attempt is made to attain it through *weight*; it then discovers itself (through an association of ideas) by a preference for a *deep register,* and (as I have had opportunity to observe) by the insinuation of a second, mysterious notion, usually of a literary sort. If these are not the sole specific signs, they are the most important ones.

To every disciple of philosophy, however, depth of feeling would seem to imply exhaustiveness in feeling, a complete absorption in the given mood.

Whoever, surrounded by the full tide of a genuine carnival crowd, slinks about morosely or even indifferently, neither affected nor carried away by the tremendous self-satire of mask and motley, by the might of misrule over law, by the vengeful feeling of wit running riot, shows himself incapable of sounding the depths of feeling. This gives further confirmation of the fact, that depth of feeling roots in a complete absorption in the given mood, however frivolous, and blossoms in the interpretation of that mood; whereas the current conception of deep feeling singles out only one aspect of feeling in man, and specializes that.

In the so-called "Champagne Aria" in Don Giovanni there lies more "depth" than in many a funeral march or nocturne:— Depth of feeling also shows in not wasting it on subordinate or unimportant matters.

9

Routine is highly esteemed and frequently required; in musical "officialdom" it is a *sine qua non*. That routine in music should exist at all, and, furthermore, that it can be nominated as a condition in the musician's bond, is another proof of the narrow confines of our musical art. Routine signifies the acquisition of a modicum of experience and artcraft, and their application to all cases which may occur; hence, there must be an astounding number of analogous cases. Now, I like to imagine a species of art-praxis wherein each case should be a new one, an exception! How helpless and impotent would the army of practical musicians stand before it!—in the end they would surely beat a retreat, and disappear. Routine transforms the temple of art into a factory. It destroys creativeness. For creation means, the bringing form out of the void; whereas routine flourishes on imitation. It is "poetry made to order." It rules because it suits the generality: In the theatre, in the orchestra, in virtuosi, in instruction. One longs to exclaim, "Avoid routine! Let each beginning be, as had none been before! Know nothing, but rather think and feel! For, behold, the myriad strains that once shall sound have existed since the beginning, ready, afloat in the æther, and together with them other myriads that shall never be heard. Only stretch forth your hands, and ye shall grasp a blossom, a breath of the sea-breeze, a sunbeam; avoid routine, for it strives to grasp only that wherewith your four walls are filled, and the same over and over again; the spirit of ease so infects you, that you will scarcely leave your armchairs, and will lay hold only of what is nearest to hand. And myriad strains are there since the beginning, still waiting for manifestation!"

"It is my misfortune, to possess no routine," Wagner once wrote Liszt, when the composition of "Tristan" was making no progress. Thus Wagner deceived himself, and wore a mask for others. He had too much routine, and his composing-machinery was thrown out of gear, just when a tangle formed in the mesh which only inspiration could unloose. True, Wagner found the clew when he succeeded in throwing off routine; but had he really never possessed it, he would have declared the fact without bitterness. And, after all, this sentence in Wagner's letter expresses the true artist-contempt for routine, inasmuch as he waives all claim to a qualification which he thinks meanly of, and takes care that others may not invest him with it. This self-praise he utters with a mien of ironic desperation. He is, in very truth, unhappy that composition is at a standstill, but finds rich consolation in the consciousness that his genius is above the cheap expedients of routine; at the same time, with an air of modesty, he sorrowfully confesses that he has not acquired a training belonging to the craft.

The sentence is a masterpiece of the native cunning of the instinct of self-preservation; but equally proves—and that is our point—the pettiness of routine in creative work.

10

Respect the Pianoforte! Its disadvantages are evident, decided, and unquestionable: The lack of sustained tone, and the pitiless, unyielding adjustment of the inalterable semitonic scale.

But its advantages and prerogatives approach the marvelous.

It gives a single man command over something complete; in its potentialities from softest to loudest in one and the same register it excels all other instruments. The trumpet can blare, but not sigh; contrariwise the flute; the pianoforte can do both. Its range embraces the highest and deepest practicable tones. Respect the Pianoforte!

Let doubters consider how the pianoforte was esteemed by Bach, Mozart, Beethoven, Liszt, who dedicated their choicest thoughts to it.

And the pianoforte has one possession wholly peculiar to itself, an inimitable device, a photograph of the sky, a ray of moonlight—the Pedal.

The effects of the pedal are unexhausted, because they have remained even to this day the drudges of a narrow-souled and senseless harmonic theory; the treatment accorded them is like trying to mould air or water into geometric forms. Beethoven, who incontestably achieved the greatest progress on and for the pianoforte, divined the mysteries of the pedal, and to him we owe the first liberties.

The pedal is in ill-repute. For this, absurd irregularities must bear the blame. Let us experiment with *sensible* irregularities.

11

"I felt . . . that the book I shall write will be neither in English nor in Latin; and this for the one reason . . . namely, that the language in which it may be given me not only to write, but also to think, will not be Latin, or English, or Italian, or Spanish, but a language not even one of whose words I know, a language in which dumb things speak to me, and in which, it may be, I shall at last have to respond in my grave to an Unknown Judge."

(Von Hoffmannsthal: A letter.)

Essays before a Sonata

Charles E. Ives

"These prefatory essays were written by the composer for those who can't stand his music—and the music for those who can't stand his essays; to those who can't stand either, the whole is respectfully dedicated."

The following pages were written primarily as a preface or reason for the [writer's] second Pianoforte Sonata—"Concord, Mass., 1845,"—a group of four pieces, called a sonata for want of a more exact name, as the form, perhaps substance, does not justify it. The music and prefaces were intended to be printed together, but as it was found that this would make a cumbersome volume they are separate. The whole is an attempt to present [one person's] impression of the spirit of transcendentalism that is associated in the minds of many with Concord, Mass., of over a half century ago. This is undertaken in impressionistic pictures of Emerson and Thoreau, a sketch of the Alcotts, and a Scherzo supposed to reflect a lighter quality which is often found in the fantastic side of Hawthorne. The first and last movements do not aim to give any programs of the life or of any particular work of either Emerson or Thoreau but rather composite pictures or impressions. They are, however, so general in outline that, from some viewpoints, they may be as far from accepted impressions (from true conceptions, for that matter) as the valuation which they purport to be of the influence of the life, thought, and character of Emerson and Thoreau is inadequate.

I Prologue

How far is anyone justified, be he an authority or a layman, in expressing or trying to express in terms of music (in sounds, if you like) the value of anything, material, moral, intellectual, or spiritual, which is usually expressed in terms other than music? How far afield can music go and keep honest as well as reasonable or artistic? Is it a matter limited only by the composer's power of expressing what lies in his subjective or objective consciousness? Or is it limited by any limitations of the composer? Can a tune literally represent a stonewall with vines on it or with nothing on it, though it (the tune) be made by a genius whose power of objective contemplation is in the highest state of development? Can it be done by anything short of an act of mesmerism on the part of the composer or an act of kindness on the part of the listener? Does the extreme materializing of music appeal strongly to anyone except to those without a sense of humor—or rather with a sense of humor?—or, except, possibly to those who might excuse it, as Herbert Spencer might by the theory that the sensational element (the sensations we hear so much about in experimental psychology) is the true pleasurable phenomenon in music and that the mind should not be allowed to interfere? Does the success of program music depend more upon the program than upon the music? If it does, what is the use of the music, if it does not, what is the use of the program? Does not its appeal depend to a great extent on the listener's willingness to accept the theory that music is the language of the emotions and *only* that? Or inversely does not this theory tend to limit music to programs?—a limitation as bad for music itself—for its wholesome progress,—as a diet of program music is bad for the listener's ability to digest anything beyond the sensuous (or physical-emotional). To a great extent this depends on what is meant by emotion or on the assumption that the word as used above refers more to the *expression, of,* rather than to a meaning in a deeper sense—which may be a feeling influenced by some experience perhaps of a spiritual nature in the expression of which the intellect has some part. "The nearer we get to the mere expression of emotion," says Professor Sturt in his *Philosophy of Art and Personality*, "as in the antics of boys who have been promised a holiday, the further we get away from art."

On the other hand is not all music, program-music,—is not pure music, so called, representative in its essence? Is it not program-music raised to the nth power or rather reduced to the minus nth power? Where is the line to be drawn between the expression of subjective and objective emotion? It is easier to know what each is than when each becomes what it is. The "Separateness of Art" theory—that art is not life but a reflection of it—"that art is not vital to life but that life is vital to it," does not help us. Nor does Thoreau who says not that "life is art," but that "life is an art," which of course is a different thing than the foregoing. Tolstoi is even more helpless to himself and to us. For he eliminates further. From his definition of art we may learn little more than that a kick in the back is a work of art, and Beethoven's 9th Symphony is not. Experiences are passed on from one man to another. Abel knew that. And now we know it. But where is the bridge placed?—at the end of the road or only at the end of our vision? Is it all a bridge?—or is there no bridge because there is no gulf? Suppose that a composer writes a piece of music conscious that he is inspired, say, by witnessing an act of great self-sacrifice—another piece by the contemplation of a certain trait of nobility he perceives in a friend's character—and another by the sight of a mountain lake under moonlight. The first two, from an inspirational standpoint would naturally seem to come under the subjective and the last under the objective, yet the chances are, there is something of the quality of both in all. There may have been in the first instance physical action so intense or so dramatic in character that the remembrance of it aroused a great deal more objective emotion than the composer was conscious of while writing the music. In the third instance, the music may have been influenced strongly though subconsciously by a vague remembrance of certain thoughts and feelings, perhaps of a deep religious or spiritual nature, which suddenly came to him upon realizing the beauty of the scene and which overpowered the first sensuous pleasure—perhaps some such feeling as of the conviction of immortality, that Thoreau experienced and tells about in *Walden*. "I penetrated to those meadows . . . when the wild river and the woods were bathed in so pure and bright a light as would have waked the dead *if* they had been slumbering in their graves as some suppose. There needs no stronger proof of immortality." Enthusiasm must permeate it, but what it is that inspires an art-effort is not easily determined much less classified. The word "inspire" is used here in the sense of cause rather than effect. A critic may say that a certain movement is not inspired. But that may be a matter of taste—perhaps the most inspired music sounds the least so—to the critic. A true inspiration may lack a true expression unless it is assumed that if an inspiration is not true enough to produce a true expression—(if there be anyone who can definitely determine what a true expression is) —it is not an inspiration at all.

Again suppose the same composer at another time writes a piece of equal merit to the other three, as estimates go; but holds that he is not conscious of what inspired it—that he had nothing definite in mind—that he was not aware of any mental image or process—that, naturally, the actual work in creating something gave him a satisfying feeling of pleasure perhaps of elation. What will you substitute for the mountain lake, for his friend's character, etc.? Will you substitute anything? If so why? If so what? Or is it enough to let the matter rest on the pleasure mainly physical, of the tones, their color, succession, and relations, formal or informal? Can an inspiration come from a blank mind? Well—he tries to explain and says that he was conscious of some emotional excitement and of a sense of something beautiful, he doesn't know exactly what—a vague feeling of exaltation or perhaps of profound sadness.

What is the source of these instinctive feelings, these vague intuitions and introspective sensations? The more we try to analyze the more vague they become. To pull them apart and classify them as "subjective" or "objective" or as this or as that, means, that they may be well classified and that is about all; it leaves us as far from the origin as ever. What does it all mean? What is behind it all? The "voice of God," says the artist, "the voice of the devil," says the man in the front row. Are we, because we are, human beings, born with the power of innate perception of the beautiful in the abstract so that an inspiration can arise through no external stimuli of sensation or experience,—no association with the outward? Or was there present in the above instance, some kind of subconscious, instantaneous, composite image, of all the mountain lakes this man had ever seen blended as kind of overtones with the various traits of nobility of many of his friends embodied in one personality? Do all inspirational images, states, conditions, or whatever they may be truly called, have for a dominant part, if not for a source, some actual experience in life or of the social relation? To think that they do not—always at least—would be a relief; but as we are trying to consider music made and heard by human beings (and not by birds or angels) it seems difficult to suppose that even subconscious images can be separated from some human experience—there must be something behind subconsciousness to produce consciousness, and so on. But whatever the elements and origin of these so-called images are, that they *do* stir deep emotional feelings and encourage their expression is a part of the unknowable we know. They do often arouse something that has not yet passed the border line between subconsciousness and consciousness—an artistic intuition (well named, but)—object and cause unknown!—here is a program!—conscious or subconscious what does it matter? Why try to trace any stream that flows through the garden of consciousness to its source only to be confronted by another problem of tracing this source to its source? Perhaps Emerson in the *Rhodora* answers by not trying to explain

> That if eyes were made for seeing
> Then beauty is its own excuse for being:
> Why thou wert there, O, rival of the rose!
> I never thought to ask, I never knew;
> But, in my simple ignorance, suppose
> The self-same Power that brought me there brought you.

Perhaps Sturt answers by substitution: "We cannot explain the origin of an artistic intuition any more than the origin of any other primary function of our nature. But if as I believe civilization is mainly founded on those kinds of unselfish human interests which we call knowledge and morality it is easily intelligible that we should have a parallel interest which we call art closely akin and lending powerful support to the other two. It is intelligible too that moral goodness, intellectual power, high vitality, and strength should be approved by the intuition." This reduces, or rather brings the problem back to a tangible basis namely:—the translation of an artistic intuition into musical sounds approving and reflecting, or endeavoring to approve and reflect, a "moral goodness," a "high vitality," etc., or any other human attribute mental, moral, or spiritual.

Can music do *more* than this? Can it *do* this? and if so who and what is to determine the degree of its failure or success? The composer, the performer (if there be any), or those who have to listen? One hearing or a century of hearings?—and if it isn't successful or if it doesn't fail what matters it?—the fear of failure need keep no one from the attempt for if the composer is sensitive he need but launch forth a countercharge of "being misunderstood" and hide behind it. A theme that the composer sets up as "moral goodness" may sound like "high vitality," to his friend and but like an outburst of "nervous weakness" or only a "stagnant pool" to those not even his enemies. Expression to a great extent is a matter of terms and terms are anyone's. The meaning of "God" may have a billion interpretations if there be that many souls in the world.

There is a moral in the "Nominalist and Realist" that will prove all sums. It runs something like this: No matter how sincere and confidential men are in trying to know or assuming that they do know each other's mood and habits of thought, the net result leaves a feeling that all is left unsaid; for the reason of their incapacity to know each other, though they use the same words. They go on from one explanation to another but things seem to stand about as they did in the beginning "because of that vicious assumption." But we would rather believe that music is beyond any analogy to word language and that the time is coming, but not in our lifetime, when it will develop possibilities unconceivable now,—a language, so transcendent, that its heights and depths will be common to all mankind.

II Emerson

1

It has seemed to the writer, that Emerson is greater—his identity more complete perhaps—in the realms of revelation—natural disclosure—than in those of poetry, philosophy, or prophecy. Though a great poet and prophet, he is greater, possibly, as an invader of the unknown,—America's deepest explorer of the spiritual immensities,—a seer painting his discoveries in masses and with any color that may lie at hand—cosmic, religious, human, even sensuous; a recorder, freely describing the inevitable struggle in the soul's uprise—perceiving from this inward source alone, that every "ultimate fact is only the first of a new series"; a discoverer, whose heart knows, with Voltaire, "that man seriously reflects when left alone," and would then discover, if he can, that "wondrous chain which links the heavens with earth—the world of beings subject to one law." In *his* reflections Emerson, unlike Plato, is not afraid to ride Arion's Dolphin, and to go wherever he is carried—to Parnassus or to "Musketaquid."

We see him standing on a summit, at the door of the infinite where many men do not care to climb, peering into the mysteries of life, contemplating the eternities, hurling back whatever he discovers there,—now, thunderbolts for us to grasp, if we can, and translate—now placing quietly, even tenderly, in our hands, things that we may see without effort—if we won't see them, so much the worse for us.

We see him,—a mountain-guide, so intensely on the lookout for the trail of his star, that he has no time to stop and retrace his footprints, which may often seem indistinct to his followers, who find it easier and perhaps safer to keep their eyes on the ground. And there is a chance that this guide could not always retrace his steps if he tried—and why should he!—he is on the road, conscious only that, though his star may not lie within walking distance, he must reach it before his wagon can be hitched to it—a Prometheus illuminating a privilege of the Gods —lighting a fuse that is laid towards men. Emerson reveals the less not by an analysis of itself, but by bringing men towards the greater. He does not try to reveal, personally, but leads, rather, to a field where revelation is a harvest-part, where it is known by the perceptions of the soul towards the absolute law. He leads us towards this law, which is a realization of what experience has suggested and philosophy hoped for. He leads us, conscious that the aspects of truth, as he sees them, may change as often as truth remains constant. Revelation perhaps, is but prophecy intensified—the intensifying of its mason-work as well as its steeple. Simple prophecy, while concerned with the past, reveals but the future, while revelation is concerned with all time. The power in Emerson's prophecy confuses it with—or at least makes it seem to approach—revelation. It is prophecy with no time element. Emerson tells, as few bards could, of what will happen in the past, for his future is eternity and the past is a part of that. And so like all true prophets, he is always modern, and will grow modern with the years—for his substance is not relative but a measure of eternal truths determined rather by a universalist than by a partialist. He measured, as Michel Angelo said true artists should, "with the eye and not the hand." But to attribute modernism to his substance, though not to his expression, is an anachronism—and as futile as calling to-day's sunset modern.

As revelation and prophecy, in their common acceptance are resolved by man, from the absolute and universal, to the relative and personal, and as Emerson's tendency is fundamentally the opposite, it is easier, safer and so apparently clearer, to think of him as a poet of natural and revealed philosophy. And as such, a prophet—but not one to be confused with those singing soothsayers, whose pockets are filled, as are the pockets of conservative-reaction and radical demagoguery in pulpit, street-corner, bank and columns, with dogmatic fortune-tellings. Emerson, as a prophet in these lower heights, was a conservative, in that he seldom lost his head, and a radical, in that he seldom cared whether he lost it or not. He was a born radical as are all true conservatives. He was too much "absorbed by the absolute," too much of the universal to be either—though he could be both at once. To Cotton Mather, he would have been a demagogue, to a real demagogue he would not be understood, as it was with no self interest that he laid his hand on reality. The nearer any subject or an attribute of it, approaches to the perfect truth at its base, the more does qualification become necessary. Radical-ism must always qualify itself. Emerson clarifies as he qualifies, by plunging into, rather than "emerging from Carlyle's soul-confusing labyrinths of speculative radicalism." The radicalism that we hear much about to-day, is not Emerson's kind—but of thinner fiber—it qualifies itself by going to *A* "root" and often cutting other roots in the process; it is usually impotent as dyna-mite in its cause and sometimes as harmful to the wholesome progress of all causes; it is qualified by its failure. But the Rad-icalism of Emerson plunges to all roots, it becomes greater than itself—greater than all its formal or informal doctrines—too ad-vanced and too conservative for any specific result—too catholic for all the churches—for the nearer it is to truth, the farther it is from a truth, and the more it is qualified by its future possibilities.

Hence comes the difficulty—the futility of attempting to fasten on Emerson any particular doctrine, philosophic, or re-ligious theory. Emerson wrings the neck of any law, that would become exclusive and arrogant, whether a definite one of meta-physics or an indefinite one of mechanics. He hacks his way up and down, as near as he can to the absolute, the oneness of all nature both human and spiritual, and to God's benevolence. To him the ultimate of a conception is its vastness, and it is prob-ably this, rather than the "blind-spots" in his expression that makes us incline to go with him but half-way; and then stand and build dogmas. But if we can not follow all the way—if we do not always clearly perceive the whole picture, we are at least free to imagine it—he makes us feel that we are free to do so; perhaps that is the most he asks. For he is but reaching out through and beyond mankind, trying to see what he can of the infinite and its immensities—throwing back to us whatever he can—but ever conscious that he but occasionally catches a glimpse; conscious that if he would contemplate the greater, he must wrestle with the lesser, even though it dims an outline; that he must struggle if he would hurl back anything—even a broken fragment for men to examine and perchance in it find a germ of some part of truth; conscious at times, of the futility of his effort and its message, conscious of its vagueness, but ever hopeful for it, and confident that its foundation, if not its medium is somewhere near the eventual and "absolute good"— the divine truth underlying all life. If Emerson must be dubbed an optimist—then an optimist fighting pessimism, but not wallowing in it; an optimist, who does not study pessimism by learning to enjoy it, whose imagination is greater than his curiosity, who seeing the sign-post to Erebus, is strong enough to go the other way. This strength of optimism, indeed the strength we find always underlying his tolerance, his radicalism, his searches, prophecies, and revelations, is heightened and made efficient by "imagination-penetrative," a thing concerned not with the combining but the apprehending of things. A possession, akin to the power, Ruskin says, all great pictures have, which "depends on the penetration of the imagination into the true nature of the thing represented, and on the scorn of the imagination for all shackles and fetters of mere external fact that stand in the way of its suggestiveness"—a possession which gives the strength of distance to his eyes, and the strength of muscle to his soul. With this he slashes down through the loam—nor would he have us rest there. If we would dig deep enough only to plant a doctrine, from one part of him, he would show us the quick-silver in that furrow. If we would creed his *Compensation,* there is hardly a sentence that could not wreck it, or could not show that the idea is no tenet of a philosophy, but a clear (though perhaps not clearly hurled on the canvas) illustration of universal justice—of God's perfect balances; a story of the analogy or better the identity of polarity and duality in Nature with that in morality. The essay is no more a doctrine than the law of gravitation is. If we would stop and attribute too much to genius, he shows us that "what is best written or done by genius in the world, was no one man's work, but came by wide social labor, when a thousand wrought like one, sharing the same impulse." If we would find in his essay on Montaigne, a biography, we are shown a biography of scepticism—and in reducing this to relation between "sensation and the morals" we are shown a true Montaigne—we know the man better perhaps by this less presentation. If we would stop and trust heavily on the harvest of originality, he shows us that this plant—this part of the garden—is but a relative thing. It is dependent also on the richness that ages have put into the soil. "Every thinker is retrospective."

Thus is Emerson always beating down through the crust towards the first fire of life, of death and of eternity. Read where you will, each sentence seems not to point to the next but to the undercurrent of all. If you would label his a religion of ethics or of morals, he shames you at the outset, "for ethics is but a reflection of a divine personality." All the religions this world has ever known, have been but the aftermath of the ethics of one or another holy person; "as soon as character appears be sure love will"; "the intuition of the moral sentiment is but the insight of the perfection of the laws of the soul"; but these laws cannot be catalogued.

If a versatilist, a modern Goethe, for instance, could put all of Emerson's admonitions into practice, a constant permanence would result,—an eternal short-circuit—a focus of equal X-rays. Even the value or success of but one precept is dependent, like that of a ball-game as much on the batting-eye as on the pitch-ing-arm. The inactivity of permanence is what Emerson will not permit. He will not accept repose against the activity of truth. But this almost constant resolution of every insight towards the absolute may get a little on one's nerves, if one is at all partial-wise to the specific; one begins to ask what is the absolute any-way, and why try to look clear through the eternities and the unknowable even out of the other end. Emerson's fondness for flying to definite heights on indefinite wings, and the tendency to over-resolve, becomes unsatisfying to the impatient, who want results to come as they walk. Probably this is a reason that it is occasionally said that Emerson has no vital message for the rank and file. He has no definite message perhaps for the literal, but messages are all vital, as much, by reason of his indefiniteness, as in spite of it.

There is a suggestion of irony in the thought that the power of his vague but compelling vitality, which ever sweeps us on in spite of ourselves, might not have been his, if it had not been for those definite religious doctrines of the old New England theologians. For almost two centuries, Emerson's mental and spiritual muscles had been in training for him in the moral and intellectual contentions, a part of the religious exercise of his forebears. A kind of higher sensitiveness seems to culminate in him. It gives him a power of searching for a wider freedom of soul than theirs. The religion of Puritanism was based to a great extent, on a search for the unknowable, limited only by the dogma of its theology—a search for a path, so that the soul could better be conducted to the next world, while Emerson's transcendentalism was based on the wider search for the unknowable, unlimited in any way or by anything except the vast bounds of innate goodness, as it might be revealed to him in any phenomena of man, Nature, or God. This distinction, tenuous, in spite of the definite-sounding words, we like to believe has something peculiar to Emerson in it. We like to feel that it superimposes the one that makes all transcendentalism but an intellectual state, based on the theory of innate ideas, the reality of thought and the necessity of its freedom. For the philosophy of the religion, or whatever you will call it, of the Concord Transcendentalists is at least, more than an intellectual state—it has even some of the functions of the Puritan church—it is a spiritual state in which both soul *and* mind can better conduct themselves in this world, and also in the next—when the time comes. The search of the Puritan was rather along the path of logic, spiritualized, and the transcendentalist of reason, spiritualized—a difference in a broad sense between objective and subjective contemplation.

The dislike of inactivity, repose and barter, drives one to the indefinite subjective. Emerson's lack of interest in permanence may cause him to present a subjectivity harsher on the outside than is essential. His very universalism occasionally seems a limitation. Somewhere here may lie a weakness—real to some, apparent to others—a weakness in so far as his relation becomes less vivid—to the many; insofar as he over-disregards the personal unit in the universal. If Genius is the most indebted, how much does it owe to those who would, but do not easily ride with it? If there is a weakness here is it the fault of substance or only of manner? If of the former, there is organic error somewhere, and Emerson will become less and less valuable to man. But this seems impossible, at least to us. Without considering his manner or expression here (it forms the general subject of the second section of this paper), let us ask if Emer-

son's substance needs an affinity, a supplement or even a complement or a gangplank? And if so, of what will it be composed?

Perhaps Emerson could not have risen to his own, if it had
not been for his Unitarian training and association with the
churchmen emancipators. "Christianity is founded on, and sup-
poses the authority of, reason, and cannot therefore oppose it,
without subverting itself." . . . "Its office is to discern universal
truths, great and eternal principles . . . the highest power of the
soul." Thus preached Channing. Who knows but this pulpit
aroused the younger Emerson to the possibilities of intuitive
reasoning in spiritual realms? The influence of men like Channing in his fight for the dignity of human nature, against the
arbitrary revelations that Calvinism had strapped on the church,
and for the belief in the divine in human reason, doubtless encouraged Emerson in his unshackled search for the infinite, and
gave him premises which he later took for granted instead of
carrying them around with him. An overinterest, not an under-
interest in Christian ideal aims, may have caused him to feel
that the definite paths were well established and doing their
share, and that for some to reach the same infinite ends, more
paths might be opened—paths which would in themselves, and
in a more transcendent way, partake of the spiritual nature of
the land in quest,—another expression of God's Kingdom in
Man. Would you have the indefinite paths *always* supplemented
by the shadow of the definite one of a first influence?

A characteristic of rebellion, is that its results are often
deepest, when the rebel breaks not from the worst to the greatest,
but from the great to the greater. The youth of the rebel in-
creases this characteristic. The innate rebellious spirit in young
men is active and buoyant. They could rebel against and im-
prove the millennium. This excess of enthusiasm at the inception
of a movement, causes loss of perspective; a natural tendency to
undervalue the great in that which is being taken as a base of
departure. A "youthful sedition" of Emerson was his withdrawal
from the communion, perhaps, the most socialistic doctrine (or
rather symbol) of the church—a "commune" above property or
class.

Picking up an essay on religion of a rather remarkable-
minded boy—perhaps with a touch of genius—written when he

was still in college, and so serving as a good illustration in point —we read—"Every thinking man knows that the church is dead." But every thinking man knows that the church-part of the church always has been dead—that part seen by candle-light, not Christ-light. Enthusiasm is restless and hasn't time to see that if the church holds itself as nothing but the symbol of the greater light it is life itself—as a symbol of a symbol it is dead. Many of the sincerest followers of Christ never heard of Him. It is the better influence of an institution that arouses in the deep and earnest souls a feeling of rebellion to make its aims more certain. It is their very sincerity that causes these seekers for a freer vision to strike down for more fundamental, universal, and perfect truths, but with such feverish enthusiasm, that they appear to overthink themselves—a subconscious way of going Godward perhaps. The rebel of the twentieth century says: "Let us discard God, immortality, miracle—but be not untrue to ourselves." Here he, no doubt, in a sincere and exalted moment, confuses God with a name. He apparently feels that there is a separatable difference between natural and revealed religion. He mistakes the powers behind them, to be fundamentally separate. In the excessive keenness of his search, he forgets that "being true to ourselves" *is* God, that the faintest thought of immortality *is* God, and that God is "miracle." Overenthusiasm keeps one from letting a common experience of a day translate what is stirring the soul. The same inspiring force that arouses the young rebel, brings later in life a kind of "experience-after-glow," a realization that the soul cannot discard or limit anything. Would you have the youthful enthusiasm of rebellion, which Emerson carried beyond his youth *always* supplemented by the shadow of experience?

Perhaps it is not the narrow minded alone that have no interest in anything, but in its relation to their personality. Is the Christian Religion, to which Emerson owes embryo-ideals, anything but the revelation of God in a personality—a revelation so that the narrow mind could become opened? But the tendency to over-personalize personality may also have suggested to Emerson the necessity for more universal, and impersonal paths, though they be indefinite of outline and vague of ascent. Could you journey, with equal benefit, if they were less so? Would you have the universal always supplemented by the shadow of the personal? If this view is accepted, and we doubt that it can be by the majority, Emerson's substance could well bear a supplement, perhaps an affinity. Something that will support that which some conceive he does not offer. Something that will help answer Alton Locke's question: "What has Emerson for the working-man?" and questions of others who look for the gang-plank before the ship comes in sight. Something that will supply the definite banister to the infinite, which it is said he keeps invisible. Something that will point a crossroad from "his personal" to "his nature." Something that may be in Thoreau or Wordsworth, or in another poet whose songs "breathe of a new morning of a higher life though a definite beauty in Nature"— or something that will show the birth of his ideal and hold out a background of revealed religion, as a perspective to his transcendent religion—a counterpoise in his rebellion—which we feel Channing or Dr. Bushnell, or other saints known and unknown might supply.

If the arc must be completed—if there are those who would have the great, dim outlines of Emerson fulfilled, it is fortunate that there are Bushnells, and Wordsworths, to whom they may appeal—to say nothing of the Vedas, the Bible, or their own souls. But such possibilities and conceptions, the deeper they are received, the more they seem to reduce their need. Emerson's Circle may be a better whole, without its complement. Perhaps his "unsatiable demand for unity, the need to recognize one nature in all variety of objects," would have been impaired, if something should make it simpler for men to find the identity they at first want in his substance. "Draw if thou canst the mystic line severing rightly his from thine, which is human, which divine." Whatever means one would use to personalize Emerson's natural revelation, whether by a vision or a board walk, the vastness of his aims and the dignity of his tolerance would doubtless cause him to accept or at least try to accept, and use "magically as a part of his fortune." He would modestly say, perhaps, "that the world is enlarged for him, not by finding new objects, but by more affinities, and potencies than those he already has." But, indeed, is not enough manifestation already there? Is not the asking that it be made more manifest forgetting that "we are not strong by our power to penetrate, but by our relatedness?" Will more signs create a greater sympathy? Is not our weak suggestion needed only for those content with their own hopelessness?

Others may lead others to him, but he finds his problem in making "gladness hope and fortitude flow from his page," rather than in arranging that our hearts be there to receive it. The first is his duty—the last ours!

2

A devotion to an end tends to undervalue the means. A power of revelation may make one more concerned about his perceptions of the soul's nature than the way of their disclosure. Emerson is more interested in what he perceives than in his expression of it. He is a creator whose intensity is consumed more with the substance of his creation than with the manner by which he shows it to others. Like Petrarch he seems more a discoverer of Beauty than an imparter of it. But these discoveries, these devotions to aims, these struggles toward the absolute, do not these in themselves, impart something, if not all, of their own unity and coherence—which is not received, as such, at first, nor is foremost in their expression. It must be remembered that "truth" was what Emerson was after——not strength of outline, or even beauty except in so far as they might reveal themselves, naturally, in his explorations towards the infinite. To think hard and deeply and to say what is thought, regardless of consequences, may produce a first impression, either of great translucence, or of great muddiness, but in the latter there may be hidden possibilities. Some accuse Brahms' orchestration of being muddy. This may be a good name for a first impression of it. But if it should seem less so, he might not be saying what he thought. The mud may be a form of sincerity which demands that the heart be translated, rather than handed around through the pit. A clearer scoring might have lowered the thought. Carlyle told Emerson that some of his paragraphs didn't cohere. Emerson wrote by sentences or phrases, rather than by logical sequence. His underlying plan of work seems based on the large unity of a series of particular aspects of a subject, rather than on the continuity of its expression. As thoughts surge to his mind, he fills the heavens with them, crowds them in, if necessary, but seldom arranges them, along the ground first. Among class-room excuses for Emerson's imperfect coherence and lack of unity, is one that remembers that his essays were made from lecture notes. His habit, often in lecturing, was to compile his ideas as they came to him on a general subject, in scattered notes, and when on the platform, to trust to the mood of the occasion, to assemble them. This seems a specious explanation, though true to fact. Vagueness, is at times, an indication of nearness to a perfect truth. The definite glory of Bernard of Cluny's Celestial City, is more beautiful than true—probably. Orderly reason does not always have to be a visible part of all great things. Logic may possibly require that unity means something ascending in self-evident relation to the parts and to the whole, with no ellipsis in the ascent. But reason may permit, even demand an ellipsis, and genius may not need the self-evident part. In fact, these parts may be the "blind-spots" in the progress of unity. They may be filled with little but repetition. "Nature loves analogy and hates repetition." Botany reveals evolution not permanence. An apparent confusion if lived with long enough may become orderly. Emerson was not writing for lazy minds, though one of the keenest of his academic friends said that, he (Emerson) could not explain many of his own pages. But why should he!—he explained them when he discovered them—the moment before he spoke or wrote them. A rare experience of a moment at daybreak, when something in nature seems to reveal all consciousness, cannot be explained at noon. Yet it is a part of the day's unity. At evening, nature is absorbed by another experience. She dislikes to explain as much as to repeat. It is conceivable, that what is unified form to the author, or composer, may of necessity be formless to his audience. A home-run will cause more unity in the grand stand than in the season's batting average. If a composer once starts to compromise, his work will begin to drag on *him*. Before the end is reached, his inspiration has all gone up in sounds pleasing to his audience, ugly to him—sacrificed for the first acoustic—an opaque clarity, a picture painted for its hanging. Easy unity, like easy virtue, is easier to describe, when judged from its lapses than from its constancy. When the infidel admits God is great, he means only: "I am lazy—it is easier to talk than live." Ruskin also says: "Suppose I like the finite curves best, who shall say I'm right or wrong? No one. It is simply a question of experience." You may not be able to experience a symphony, even after twenty performances. Initial coherence to-day may be dullness to-morrow probably because formal or outward unity depends so much on repetition, sequences, antitheses, paragraphs with inductions and summaries. Macaulay had that kind of unity. Can you read him to-day? Emerson rather goes out and shouts: "I'm thinking of the sun's glory to-day and I'll let his light shine through me. I'll say any damn thing that this inspires me with." Perhaps there are flashes of light, still in cipher, kept there by unity, the code of which the world has not yet discovered. The unity of one sentence inspires the unity of the whole—though its physique is as ragged as the *Dolomites*.

Intense lights—vague shadows—great pillars in a horizon are difficult things to nail signboards to. Emerson's outward-inward qualities make him hard to classify, but easy for some. There are many who like to say that he—even all the Concord men—are intellectuals. Perhaps—but intellectuals who wear their brains nearer the heart than some of their critics. It is as dangerous to determine a characteristic by manner as by mood. Emerson is a pure intellectual to those who prefer to take him as literally as they can. There are reformers, and in "the form" lies their interest, who prefer to stand on the plain, and then insist they see from the summit. Indolent legs supply the strength of eye for their inspiration. The intellect is never a whole. It is where the soul finds things. It is often the only track to the over-values. It appears a whole—but never becomes one even in the stock exchange, or the convent, or the laboratory. In the cleverest criminal, it is but a way to a low ideal. It can never discard the other part of its duality—the soul or the void where the soul ought to be. So why classify a quality always so relative that it is more an agency than substance; a quality that disappears when classified. "The life of the All must stream through us to make the man and the moment great." A sailor with a precious cargo doesn't analyze the water.

Because Emerson had generations of Calvinistic sermons in his blood, some cataloguers, would localize or provincialize him, with the sternness of the old Puritan mind. They make him *that*, hold him *there*. They lean heavily on what they find of the above influence in him. They won't follow the rivers in his thought and the play of his soul. And their cousin cataloguers put him in another pigeon-hole. They label him "ascetic." They translate his outward serenity into an impression of severity. But truth keeps one from being hysterical. Is a demagogue a friend of the people because he will lie to them to make them cry and raise false hopes? A search for perfect truths throws out a beauty more spiritual than sensuous. A sombre dignity of style is often confused by under-imagination and by surface-sentiment, with austerity. If Emerson's manner is not always beautiful in accordance with accepted standards, why not accept a few other standards? He is an ascetic, in that he refuses to compromise content with manner. But a real ascetic is an extremist who has but one height. Thus may come the confusion, of one who says that Emerson carries him high, but then leaves him always at *that* height—no higher—a confusion, mistaking a latent exultation for an ascetic reserve. The rules of Thorough Bass can be applied to his scale of flight no more than they can to the planetary system. Jadassohn, if Emerson were literally a composer, could no more analyze his harmony than a guide-to-Boston could. A microscope might show that he uses chords of the 9th, 11th, or the 99th, but a lens far different tells us they are used with different aims from those of Debussy. Emerson is definite in that his art is based on something stronger than the amusing or at its best the beguiling of a few mortals. If he uses a sensuous chord, it is not for sensual ears. His harmonies may float, if the wind blows in that direction, through a voluptuous atmosphere, but he has not Debussy's fondness for trying to blow a sensuous atmosphere from his own voluptuous cheeks. And so he is an ascetic! There is a distance between jowl and soul—and it is not measured by the fraction of an inch between Concord and Paris. On the other hand, if one thinks that his harmony contains no dramatic chords, because no theatrical sound is heard, let him listen to the finale of "Success," or of "Spiritual Laws," or to some of the poems, "Brahma" or "Sursum Corda," for example. Of a truth his Codas often seem to crystallize in a dramatic, though serene and sustained way, the truths of his subject—they become more active and intense, but quieter and deeper.

Then there comes along another set of cataloguers. They put him down as a "classicist," or a romanticist, or an eclectic. Because a prophet is a child of romanticism—because revelation is classic, because eclecticism quotes from eclectic Hindu Philosophy, a more sympathetic cataloguer may say, that Emerson inspires courage of the quieter kind and delight of the higher kind.

The same well-bound school teacher who told the boys that Thoreau was a naturalist because he didn't like to work, puts down Emerson as a "classic," and Hawthorne as a "romantic." A loud voice made this doubly *true* and *sure* to be on the examination paper. But this teacher of "truth *and* dogma" apparently forgot that there is no such thing as "classicism or romanticism." One has but to go to the various definitions of these to know that. If you go to a classic definition you know what a true classic is, and similarly a "true romantic." But if you go to both, you have an algebraic formula, $x = x$, a cancellation, an *aperçu*, and hence satisfying; if you go to all definitions you have another formula $x > x$, a destruction, another *aperçu*, and hence satisfying. Professor Beers goes to the dictionary (you wouldn't think a college professor would be as reckless as that). And so he can say that "romantic" is "pertaining to the style of the Christian and popular literature of the Middle Ages,"— a Roman Catholic mode of salvation (not this definition but having a definition). And so Prof. B. can say that Walter Scott is a romanticist (and Billy Phelps a classic—sometimes). But for our part Dick Croker is a classic and Job a romanticist. Another professor, Babbitt by name, links up Romanticism with Rousseau, and charges against it many of man's troubles. He somehow likes to mix it up with sin. He throws saucers at it, but in a scholarly, interesting, sincere, and accurate way. He uncovers a deformed foot, gives it a name, from which we are allowed to infer that the covered foot is healthy and named classicism. But no Christian Scientist can prove that Christ never had a stomach ache. The *Architecture of Humanism*[1] tells us that "romanti-cism consists of . . . a poetic sensibility towards the remote, as such." But is Plato a classic or towards the remote? Is Classicism a poor relation of time—not of man? Is a thing classic or roman-tic because it is or is not passed by that biologic—that indescrib-able stream-of-change going on in all life? Let us settle the point for "good," and say that a thing is classic if it is thought of in terms of the past and romantic if thought of in terms of the future—and a thing thought of in terms of the present is—well, that is impossible! Hence, we allow ourselves to say, that Emerson is neither a classic or romantic but both—and both not only at different times in one essay, but at the same time in one sentence—in one word. And must we admit it, so is everyone. If you don't believe it, there must be some true definition you haven't seen. Chopin shows a few things that Bach forgot—but he is not eclectic, they say. Brahms shows many things that Bach did remember, so he is an eclectic, they say. Leoncavallo writes pretty verses and Palestrina is a priest, and Confucius in-spires Scriabin. A choice is freedom. Natural selection is but one of Nature's tunes. "All melodious poets shall be hoarse as street ballads, when once the penetrating keynote of nature and spirit is sounded—the earth-beat, sea-beat, heart-beat, which make the tune to which the sun rolls, and the globule of blood and the sap of the trees."

An intuitive sense of values, tends to make Emerson use social, political, and even economic phenomena, as means of expression, as the accidental notes in his scale—rather than as ends, even lesser ends. In the realization that they are essential parts of the greater values, he does not confuse them with each other. He remains undisturbed except in rare instances, when the lower parts invade and seek to displace the higher. He was not afraid to say that "there are laws which should not be too well obeyed." To him, slavery was *not* a social or a political or an economic question, nor even one of morals or of ethics, but one of universal spiritual freedom only. It mattered little what party, or what platform, or what law of commerce governed men. Was man governing himself? Social error and virtue were but relative.

[1] Geoffrey Scott (Constable & Co.)

This habit of not being hindered by using, but still going beyond the great truths of living, to the greater truths of life gave force to his influence over the materialists. Thus he seems to us more a regenerator than a reformer—more an interpreter of life's reflexes than of life's facts, perhaps. Here he appears greater than Voltaire or Rousseau and helped, perhaps, by the centrality of his conceptions, he could arouse the deeper spiritual and moral emotions, without causing his listeners to distort their physical ones. To prove that mind is over matter, he doesn't place matter over mind. He is not like the man who, because he couldn't afford both, gave up metaphysics for an automobile, and when he ran over a man blamed metaphysics. He would not have us get over-excited about physical disturbance but have it accepted as a part of any progress in culture, moral, spiritual or æsthetic. If a poet retires to the mountain-side, to avoid the vulgar unculture of men, and their physical disturbance, so that he may better catch a nobler theme for his symphony, Emerson tells him that "man's culture can spare nothing, wants all material, converts all impediments into instruments, all enemies into power." The latest product of man's culture—the aeroplane, then sails o'er the mountain and instead of an inspiration—a spray of tobacco-juice falls on the poet. "Calm yourself, Poet!" says Emerson, "culture will convert furies into muses and hells into benefit. This wouldn't have befallen you if it hadn't been for the latest transcendent product of the genius of culture" (we won't say what kind), a consummation of the dreams of poets, from David to Tennyson. Material progress is but a means of expression. Realize that man's coarseness has its future and will also be refined in the gradual uprise. Turning the world upside down may be one of its lesser incidents. It is the cause, seldom the effect that interests Emerson. He can help the cause—the effect must help itself. He might have said to those who talk knowingly about the cause of war—or of the last war, and who would trace it down through long vistas of cosmic, political, moral evolution and what not—he might say that the cause of it was as simple as that of any dog-fight—the "hog-mind" of the minority against the universal mind, the majority. The un-courage of the former fears to believe in the innate goodness of mankind. The cause is always the same, the effect different by chance; it is as easy for a hog, even a stupid one, to step on a box of matches under a tenement with a thousand souls, as under an empty bird-house. The many kindly burn up for the few; for the minority is selfish and the majority generous. The minority has ruled the world for physical reasons. The physical reasons are being removed by this "converting culture." Webster will not much longer have to grope for the mind of his constituency. The majority—the people—will need no intermediary. Governments will pass from the representative to the direct. The hog-mind is the principal thing that is making this transition slow. The biggest prop to the hog-mind is pride—pride in property and the power property gives. Ruskin backs this up—"it is at the bottom of all great mistakes; other passions do occasional good, but whenever pride puts in its word . . . it is all over with the artist." The hog-mind and its handmaidens in disorder, superficial brightness, fundamental dullness, then cowardice and suspicion—all a part of the minority (the non-people) the antithesis of everything called soul, spirit, Christianity, truth, freedom—will give way more and more to the great primal truths—that there is more good than evil, that God is on the side of the majority (the people)—that he is not enthusiastic about the minority (the non-people)—that he has made men greater than man, that he has made the universal mind and the over-soul greater and a part of the individual mind and soul—that he has made the Divine a part of all.

Again, if a picture in economics is before him, Emerson plunges down to the things that *are* because they are *better* than they are. If there is a row, which there usually is, between the ebb and flood tide, in the material ocean—for example, between the theory of the present order of competition, and of attractive and associated labor, he would sympathize with Ricardo, perhaps, that labor is the measure of value, but "embrace, as do generous minds, the proposition of labor shared by all." He would go deeper than political economics, strain out the self-factor from both theories, and make the measure of each pretty much the same, so that the natural (the majority) would win, but not to the disadvantage of the minority (the artificial) because this has disappeared—it is of the majority. John Stuart Mill's political economy is losing value because it was written by a mind more "a banker's" than a "poet's." The poet knows that there is no such thing as the perpetual law of supply and demand, perhaps not of demand and supply—or of the wage-fund, or price-level, or increments earned or unearned; and that the existence of personal or public property may not prove the existence of God.

Emerson seems to use the great definite interests of humanity to express the greater, indefinite, spiritual values—to fulfill what he can in his realms of revelation. Thus, it seems that so close a relation exists between his content and expression, his substance and manner, that if he were more definite in the latter he would lose power in the former,—perhaps some of those occasional flashes would have been unexpressed—flashes that have gone down through the world and will flame on through the ages—flashes that approach as near the Divine as Beethoven in his most inspired moments—flashes of transcendent beauty, of such universal import, that they may bring, of a sudden, some intimate personal experience, and produce the same indescribable effect that comes in rare instances, to men, from some common sensation. In the early morning of a Memorial Day, a boy is awakened by martial music—a village band is marching down the street, and as the strains of Reeves' majestic *Seventh Regiment March* come nearer and nearer, he seems of a sudden translated—a moment of vivid power comes, a consciousness of material nobility, an exultant something gleaming with the possibilities of this life, an assurance that nothing is impossible, and that the whole world lies at his feet. But as the band turns the corner, at the soldiers' monument, and the march steps of the Grand Army become fainter and fainter, the boy's vision slowly vanishes—his "world" becomes less and less probable—but the experience ever lies within him in its reality. Later in life, the same boy hears the Sabbath morning bell ringing out from the white steeple at the "Center," and as it draws him to it, through the autumn fields of sumach and asters, a Gospel hymn of simple devotion comes out to him—"There's a wideness in God's mercy"—an instant suggestion of that Memorial Day morning comes—but the moment is of deeper import—there is no personal exultation—no intimate world vision—no magnified personal hope—and in their place a profound sense of a spiritual truth,—a sin within reach of forgiveness—and as the hymn voices die away, there lies at his feet—not the world, but the figure of the Saviour—he sees an unfathomable courage, an immortality for the lowest, the vastness in humility, the kindness of the human heart, man's noblest strength, and he knows that God is nothing—nothing but love! Whence cometh the wonder of a moment? From sources we know not. But we do know that from obscurity, and from this higher Orpheus come measures of sphere melodies[1] flowing in wild, native tones, ravaging the souls of men, flowing now with thousand-fold accompaniments and rich symphonies through all our hearts; modulating and divinely leading them.

3

What is character? In how far does it sustain the soul or the soul it? Is it a part of the soul? And then—what is the soul? Plato knows but cannot tell us. Every new-born man knows, but no one tells us. "Nature will not be disposed of easily. No power of genius has ever yet had the smallest success in explaining existence. The perfect enigma remains." As every blind man sees the sun, so character may be the part of the soul we, the blind, can see, and then have the right to imagine that the soul is each man's share of God, and character the muscle which tries to reveal its mysteries—a kind of its first visible radiance—the right to know that it is the voice which is always calling the pragmatist a fool.

At any rate, it can be said that Emerson's character has much to do with his power upon us. Men who have known nothing of his life, have borne witness to this. It is directly at the root of his substance, and affects his manner only indirectly. It gives the sincerity to the constant spiritual hopefulness we are always conscious of, and which carries with it often, even when the expression is somber, a note of exultation in the victories of "the innate virtues" of man. And it is this, perhaps, that makes us feel his courage—not a self-courage, but a sympathetic one—courageous even to tenderness. It is the open courage of a

---

[1] Paraphrased from a passage in *Sartor Resartus*.

kind heart, of not forcing opinions—a thing much needed when the cowardly, underhanded courage of the fanatic would *force* opinion. It is the courage of believing in freedom, per se, rather than of trying to force everyone to *see* that you believe in it—the courage of the willingness to be reformed, rather than of reforming—the courage teaching that sacrifice is bravery, and force, fear. The courage of righteous indignation, of stammering eloquence, of spiritual insight, a courage ever contracting or unfolding a philosophy as it grows—a courage that would make the impossible possible. Oliver Wendell Holmes says that Emerson attempted the impossible in the *Over-Soul*—"an overflow of spiritual imagination." But he (Emerson) accomplished the impossible in attempting it, and still leaving it impossible. A courageous struggle to satisfy, as Thoreau says, "Hunger rather than the palate"—the hunger of a lifetime sometimes by one meal. His essay on the Pre-Soul (which he did not write) treats of that part of the over-soul's influence on unborn ages, and attempts the impossible only when it stops attempting it.

Like all courageous souls, the higher Emerson soars, the more lowly he becomes. "Do you think the porter and the cook have no experiences, no wonders for you? Everyone knows as much as the Savant." To some, the way to be humble is to admonish the humble, not learn from them. Carlyle would have Emerson teach by more definite signs, rather than interpret his revelations, or shall we say preach? Admitting all the inspiration and help that *Sartor Resartus* has given in spite of its vaudeville and tragic stages, to many young men getting under way in the life of tailor or king, we believe it can be said (but very broadly said) that Emerson, either in the first or second series of essays, taken as a whole, gives, it seems to us, greater inspiration, partly because his manner is less didactic, less personally suggestive, perhaps less clearly or obviously human than Carlyle's. How direct this inspiration is is a matter of personal viewpoint, temperament, perhaps inheritance. Augustine Birrell says he does not feel it—and he seems not to even indirectly. Apparently "a non-sequacious author" can't inspire him, for Emerson seems to him a "little thin and vague." Is Emerson or the English climate to blame for this? He, Birrell, says a really great author dissipates all fears as to his staying power. (Though fears for our staying-power, not Emerson's, is what we would like dissipated.) Besides, around a really great author, there are no fears to dissipate. "A wise author never allows his reader's mind to be at large," but Emerson is not a *wise* author. His essay on Prudence has nothing to do with prudence, for to be wise and prudent he must put explanation first, and let his substance dissolve because of it. "How carefully," says Birrell again, "a really great author like Dr. Newman, or M. Renan, explains to you what he is going to do, and how he is going to do it." Personally we like the chance of having a hand in the "explaining." We prefer to look at flowers, but not through a botany, for it seems that if we look at them alone, we see a beauty of Nature's poetry, a direct gift from the Divine, and if we look at botany alone, we see the beauty of Nature's intellect, a direct gift of the Divine—if we look at both together, we see nothing.

Thus it seems that Carlyle and Birrell would have it that courage and humility have something to do with "explanation" —and that it is not "a respect for all"—a faith in the power of "innate virtue" to perceive by "relativeness rather than pene-tration"—that causes Emerson to withhold explanation to a greater degree than many writers. Carlyle asks for more utility, and Birrell for more inspiration. But we like to believe that it is the height of Emerson's character, evidenced especially in his courage and humility that shades its quality, rather than that its virtue is less—that it is his height that will make him more and more valuable and more and more within the reach of all— whether it be by utility, inspiration, or other needs of the human soul.

Cannot some of the most valuable kinds of utility and inspiration come from humility in its highest and purest forms? For is not the truest kind of humility a kind of glorified or transcendent democracy—the practicing it rather than the talk-ing it—the not-wanting to level all finite things, but the being willing to be leveled towards the infinite? Until humility pro-duces that frame of mind and spirit in the artist can his audience gain the greatest kind of utility and inspiration, which might be quite invisible at first? Emerson realizes the value of "*the many*,"—that the law of averages has a divine source. He recog-nizes the various life-values *in reality*—not by reason of their closeness or remoteness, but because he sympathizes with men who live them, and the *majority* do. "The private store of reason is not great—would that there were a public store for man," cries Pascal, but there is, says Emerson, it is the universal mind, an institution congenital with the common or over-soul. Pascal is discouraged, for he lets himself be influenced by surface political and religious history which shows the struggle of the group, led by an individual, rather than that of the individual led by himself—a struggle as much privately caused as privately led. The main-path of all social progress has been spiritual rather than intellectual in character, but the many by-paths of individual-materialism, though never obliterating the highway, have dimmed its outlines and caused travelers to confuse the colors along the road. A more natural way of freeing the congestion in the benefits of material progress will make it less difficult for the majority to recognize the true relation between the important spiritual and religious values and the less important intellectual and economic values. As the action of the intellect and universal mind becomes more and more identical, the clearer will the relation of all values become. But for physical reasons, the group has had to depend upon the individual as leaders, and the leaders with few exceptions restrained the universal mind—they trusted to the "private store," but now, thanks to the lessons of evolution, which Nature has been teaching men since and before the days of Socrates, the public store of reason is gradually taking the place of the once-needed leader. From the Chaldean tablet to the wireless message this public store has been wonderfully opened. The results of these lessons, the possibilities they are offering for ever coordinating the mind of humanity, the culmination of this age-instruction, are seen to-day in many ways. Labor Federation, Suffrage Extension, are two instances that come to mind among the many. In these manifestations, by reason of tradition, or the bad-habit part of tradition, the hog-mind of the few (the minority), comes in play. The possessors of this are called leaders, but even these "thick-skins" are beginning to see that the *movement* is the leader, and that they are only clerks. Broadly speaking, the effects evidenced in the political side of history have so much of the physical because the causes have been so much of the physical. As a result the leaders for the most part have been under-average men, with skins thick, wits slick, and hands quick with under-values, otherwise they would not have become leaders. But the day of leaders, as such, is gradually closing—the people are beginning to lead themselves—the public store of reason is slowly being opened—the common universal mind and the common over-soul is slowly but inevitably coming into its own. "Let a man believe in God, not in names and places and persons. Let the great soul incarnated in some poor . . . sad and simple Joan, go out to service and sweep chimneys and scrub floors . . . its effulgent day beams cannot be muffled . . ." and then "to sweep and scrub will instantly appear supreme and beautiful actions . . . and *all* people will get brooms and mops." Perhaps, if all of Emerson—his works and his life—were to be swept away, and nothing of him but the record of the following incident remained to men—the influence of his soul would still be great. A working woman after coming from one of his lectures said: "I love to go to hear Emerson, not because I understand him, but because he looks as though he thought everybody was as good as he was." Is it not the courage—the spiritual hopefulness in his humility that makes this story possible and true? Is it not this trait in his character that sets him above all creeds—that gives him inspired belief in the common mind and soul? Is it not this courageous universalism that gives conviction to his prophecy and that makes his symphonies of revelation begin and end with nothing but the strength and beauty of innate goodness in man, in Nature and in God, the greatest and most inspiring theme of Concord Transcendental Philosophy, as we hear it.

And it is from such a world-compelling theme and from such vantage ground, that Emerson rises to almost perfect freedom of action, of thought and of soul, in any direction and to any height. A vantage ground, somewhat vaster than Schelling's conception of transcendental philosophy—"a philosophy of Nature become subjective." In Concord it *includes* the objective and becomes subjective to nothing but freedom and the absolute law. It is this underlying courage of the purest humility that gives Emerson that outward aspect of serenity which is felt to so great an extent in much of his work, especially in his codas and perorations. And within this poised strength, we are conscious of that "original authentic fire" which Emerson missed in Shelley—we are conscious of something that is not dispassionate, something that is at times almost turbulent—a kind of furious calm lying deeply in the conviction of the eventual triumph of the soul and its union with God!

Let us place the transcendent Emerson where he, himself, places Milton, in Wordsworth's apostrophe: "Pure as the naked heavens, majestic, free, so didst thou travel on life's common way in cheerful Godliness."

The Godliness of spiritual courage and hopefulness—these fathers of faith rise to a glorified peace in the depth of his greater perorations. There is an "oracle" at the beginning of the *Fifth Symphony*—in those four notes lies one of Beethoven's greatest messages. We would place its translation above the relentlessness of fate knocking at the door, above the greater human-message of destiny, and strive to bring it towards the spiritual message of Emerson's revelations—even to the "common heart" of Concord—the Soul of humanity knocking at the door of the Divine mysteries, radiant in the faith that it *will* be opened —and the human become the Divine!

III   Hawthorne

The substance of Hawthorne is so dripping wet with the supernatural, the phantasmal, the mystical—so surcharged with adventures, from the deeper picturesque to the illusive fantastic, one unconsciously finds oneself thinking of him as a poet of greater imaginative impulse than Emerson or Thoreau. He was not a greater poet possibly than they—but a greater artist. Not only the character of his substance, but the care in his manner throws his workmanship, in contrast to theirs, into a kind of bas-relief. Like Poe he quite naturally and unconsciously reaches out over his subject to his reader. His mesmerism seeks to mesmerize us—beyond Zenobia's sister. But he is too great an artist to show his hand "in getting his audience," as Poe and Tschaikowsky occasionally do. His intellectual muscles are too strong to let him become over-influenced, as Ravel and Stravinsky seem to be by the morbidly fascinating—a kind of false beauty obtained by artistic monotony. However, we cannot but feel that he would weave his spell over us—as would the Grimms and Æsop. We feel as much under magic as the "Enchanted Frog." This is part of the artist's business. The effect is a part of his art-effort in its inception. Emerson's substance and even his manner has little to do with a designed effect—his thunderbolts or delicate fragments are flashed out regardless— they may knock us down or just spatter us—it matters little to him—but Hawthorne is more considerate; that is, he is more artistic, as men say.

Hawthorne may be more noticeably indigenous or may have more local color, perhaps more national color than his Concord contemporaries. But the work of anyone who is somewhat more interested in psychology than in transcendental philosophy, will weave itself around individuals and their personalities. If the same anyone happens to live in Salem, his work is likely to be colored by the Salem wharves and Salem witches. If the same anyone happens to live in the "Old Manse" near the Concord Battle Bridge, he is likely "of a rainy day to betake himself to the huge garret," the secrets of which he wonders at, "but is too reverent of their dust and cobwebs to disturb." He is likely to "bow below the shriveled canvas of an old (Puritan) clergyman in wig and gown—the parish priest of a century ago—a friend of Whitefield." He is likely to come under the spell of this reverend Ghost who haunts the "Manse" and as it rains and darkens and the sky glooms through the dusty attic windows, he is likely "to muse deeply and wonderingly upon the humiliating fact that the works of man's intellect decay like those of his hands" . . . "that thought grows moldy," and as the garret is in Massachusetts, the "thought" and the "mold" are likely to be quite native. When the same anyone puts his poetry into novels rather than essays, he is likely to have more to say about the life around him—about the inherited mystery of the town—than a poet of philosophy is.

In Hawthorne's usual vicinity, the atmosphere was charged with the somber errors and romance of eighteenth century New England,—ascetic or noble New England as you like. A novel, of necessity, nails an art-effort down to some definite part or parts of the earth's surface—the novelist's wagon can't always be hitched to a star. To say that Hawthorne was more deeply interested than some of the other Concord writers—Emerson, for example—in the idealism peculiar to his native land (in so far as such idealism of a country can be conceived of as separate from the political) would be as unreasoning as to hold that he was more interested in social progress than Thoreau, because he was in the consular service and Thoreau was in no one's service—or that the War Governor of Massachusetts was a greater patriot than Wendell Phillips, who was ashamed of all political parties. Hawthorne's art was true and typically American—as is the art of all men living in America who believe in freedom of thought and who live wholesome lives to prove it, whatever their means of expression.

Any comprehensive conception of Hawthorne, either in words or music, must have for its basic theme something that has to do with the influence of sin upon the conscience—something more than the Puritan conscience, but something which is permeated by it. In this relation he is wont to use what Hazlitt calls the "moral power of imagination." Hawthorne would try to spiritualize a guilty conscience. He would sing of the relentlessness of guilt, the inheritance of guilt, the shadow of guilt darkening innocent posterity. All of its sins and morbid horrors, its specters, its phantasmas, and even its hellish hopelessness play around his pages, and vanishing between the lines are the less guilty Elves of the Concord Elms, which Thoreau and Old Man Alcott may have felt, but knew not as intimately as Hawthorne. There is often a pervading melancholy about Hawthorne, as Faguet says of de Musset "without posture, without noise but penetrating." There is at times the mysticism and serenity of the ocean, which Jules Michelet sees in "its horizon rather than in its waters." There is a sensitiveness to supernatural sound waves. Hawthorne feels the mysteries and tries to paint them rather than explain them—and here, some may say that he is wiser in a more practical way and so more artistic than Emerson. Perhaps so, but no greater in the deeper ranges and profound mysteries of the interrelated worlds of human and spiritual life.

This fundamental part of Hawthorne is not attempted in

our music (the 2d movement of the series) which is but an "extended fragment" trying to suggest some of his wilder, fantastical adventures into the half-childlike, half-fairylike phantasmal realms. It may have something to do with the children's excitement on that "frosty Berkshire morning, and the frost imagery on the enchanted hall window" or something to do with "Feathertop," the "Scarecrow," and his "Looking Glass" and the little demons dancing around his pipe bowl; or something to do with the old hymn tune that haunts the church and sings only to those in the churchyard, to protect them from secular noises, as when the circus parade comes down Main Street; or something to do with the concert at the Stamford camp meeting, or the "Slave's Shuffle"; or something to do with the Concord he-nymph, or the "Seven Vagabonds," or "Circe's Palace," or something else in the wonderbook—not something that happens, but the way something happens; or something to do with the "Celestial Railroad," or "Phœbe's Garden," or something personal, which tries to be "national" suddenly at twilight, and universal suddenly at midnight; or something about the ghost of a man who never lived, or about something that never will happen, or something else that is not.

IV   "The Alcotts"

If the dictagraph had been perfected in Bronson Alcott's time, he might now be a great writer. As it is, he goes down as Concord's greatest talker. "Great expecter," says Thoreau; "great feller," says Sam Staples, "for talkin' big . . . but his daughters is the gals though—always *doin'* somethin'." Old Man Alcott, however, was usually "doin' somethin' " within. An internal grandiloquence made him melodious without; an exuberant, irrepressible, visionary absorbed with philosophy *as* such; to him it was a kind of transcendental business, the profits of which supported his inner man rather than his family. Apparently his deep interest in spiritual physics, rather than metaphysics, gave a kind of hypnotic mellifluous effect to his voice when he sang his oracles; a manner something of a cross between an inside pompous self-assertion and an outside serious benevolence. But he was sincere and kindly intentioned in his eagerness to extend what he could of the better influence of the philosophic world as he saw it. In fact, there is a strong didactic streak in both father and daughter. Louisa May seldom misses a chance to bring out the moral of a homely virtue. The power of repetition was to them a natural means of illustration. It is said that the elder Alcott, while teaching school, would frequently whip himself when the scholars misbehaved, to show that the Divine Teacher—God—was pained when his children of the earth were bad. Quite often the boy next to the bad boy was punished, to show how sin involved the guiltless. And Miss Alcott is fond of working her story around, so that she can better rub in a moral precept—and the moral sometimes browbeats the story. But with all the elder Alcott's vehement, impracticable, visionary qualities, there was a sturdiness and a courage —at least, we like to think so. A Yankee boy who would cheerfully travel in those days, when distances were long and unmotored, as far from Connecticut as the Carolinas, earning his way by peddling, laying down his pack to teach school when opportunity offered, must possess a basic sturdiness. This was apparently not very evident when he got to preaching his idealism. An incident in Alcott's life helps confirm a theory—not a popular one—that men accustomed to wander around in the visionary unknown are the quickest and strongest when occasion requires ready action of the lower virtues. It often appears that a contemplative mind is more capable of action than an actively objective one. Dr. Emerson says: "It is good to know that it has been recorded of Alcott, the benign idealist, that when the Rev. Thomas Wentworth Higginson, heading the rush on the U. S. Court House in Boston, to rescue a fugitive slave, looked back for his following at the court-room door, only the apostolic philosopher was there cane in hand." So it seems that his idealism had some substantial virtues, even if he couldn't make a living.

The daughter does not accept the father as a prototype—she seems to have but few of her father's qualities "in female." She supported the family and at the same time enriched the lives of a large part of young America, starting off many little minds with wholesome thoughts and many little hearts with wholesome emotions. She leaves memory-word-pictures of healthy, New England childhood days,—pictures which are turned to with affection by middle-aged children,—pictures, that bear a sentiment, a leaven, that middle-aged America needs nowadays more than we care to admit.

Concord village, itself, reminds one of that common virtue lying at the height and root of all the Concord divinities. As one walks down the broad-arched street, passing the white house of Emerson—ascetic guard of a former prophetic beauty—he comes presently beneath the old elms overspreading the Alcott house. It seems to stand as a kind of homely but beautiful witness of Concord's common virtue—it seems to bear a consciousness that its past *is living*, that the "mosses of the Old Manse" and the hickories of Walden are not far away. Here is the home of the "Marches"—all pervaded with the trials and happiness of the family and telling, in a simple way, the story of "the richness of not having." Within the house, on every side, lie remembrances of what imagination can do for the better amusement of fortunate children who have to do for themselves—much-needed lessons in these days of automatic, ready-made, easy entertainment which deaden rather than stimulate the creative faculty. And there sits the little old spinet-piano Sophia Thoreau gave to the Alcott children, on which Beth played the old Scotch airs, and played at the *Fifth Symphony*.

There is a commonplace beauty about "Orchard House"—a kind of spiritual sturdiness underlying its quaint picturesqueness—a kind of common triad of the New England homestead, whose overtones tell us that there must have been something æsthetic fibered in the Puritan severity—the self-sacrificing part of the ideal—a value that seems to stir a deeper feeling, a stronger sense of being nearer some perfect truth than a Gothic cathedral or an Etruscan villa. All around you, under the Concord sky, there still floats the influence of that human faith melody, transcendent and sentimental enough for the enthusiast or the cynic respectively, reflecting an innate hope—a common interest in common things and common men—a tune the Concord bards are ever playing, while they pound away at the immensities with a Beethovenlike sublimity, and with, may we say, a vehemence and perseverance—for that part of greatness is not so difficult to emulate.

We dare not attempt to follow the philosophic raptures of Bronson Alcott—unless you will assume that his apotheosis will show how "practical" his vision in this world would be in the next. And so we won't try to reconcile the music sketch of the Alcotts with much besides the memory of that home under the elms—the Scotch songs and the family hymns that were sung at the end of each day—though there may be an attempt to catch something of that common sentiment (which we have tried to suggest above)—a strength of hope that never gives way to despair—a conviction in the power of the common soul which, when all is said and done, may be as typical as any theme of Concord and its transcendentalists.

V Thoreau

Thoreau was a great musician, not because he played the flute but because he did not have to go to Boston to hear "the Symphony." The rhythm of his prose, were there nothing else, would determine his value as a composer. He was divinely conscious of the enthusiasm of Nature, the emotion of her rhythms and the harmony of her solitude. In this consciousness he sang of the submission to Nature, the religion of contemplation, and the freedom of simplicity—a philosophy distinguishing between the complexity of Nature which teaches freedom, and the complexity of materialism which teaches slavery. In music, in poetry, in all art, the truth as one sees it must be given in terms which bear some proportion to the inspiration. In their greatest moments the inspiration of both Beethoven and Thoreau express profound truths and deep sentiment, but the intimate passion of it, the storm and stress of it, affected Beethoven in such a way that he could not but be ever showing it and Thoreau that he could not easily expose it. They were equally imbued with it, but with different results. A difference in temperament had something to do with this, together with a difference in the quality of expression between the two arts. "Who that has heard a strain of music feared lest he would speak extravagantly forever," says Thoreau. Perhaps music is the art of speaking extravagantly. Herbert Spencer says that some men, as for instance Mozart, are so peculiarly sensitive to emotion . . . that music is to them but a continuation not only of the expression but of the actual emotion, though the theory of some more modern thinkers in the philosophy of art doesn't always bear this out. However, there is no doubt that in its nature music is predominantly subjective and tends to subjective expression, and poetry more objective tending to objective expression. Hence the poet when his muse calls for a deeper feeling must invert this order, and he may be reluctant to do so as these depths often call for an intimate expression which the physical looks of the words may repel. They tend to reveal the nakedness of his soul rather than its warmth. It is not a matter of the relative value of the aspiration, or a difference between subconsciousness and consciousness but a difference in the arts themselves; for example, a composer may not shrink from having the public hear his "love letter in tones," while a poet may feel sensitive about having everyone read his "letter in words." When the object of the love is mankind the sensitiveness is changed only in degree.

But the message of Thoreau, though his fervency may be inconstant and his human appeal not always direct, is, both in thought and spirit, as universal as that of any man who ever wrote or sang—as universal as it is nontemporaneous—as universal as it is free from the measure of history, as "solitude is free from the measure of the miles of space that intervene between man and his fellows." In spite of the fact that Henry James (who knows almost everything) says that "Thoreau is more than provincial—that he is parochial," let us repeat that Henry Thoreau, in respect to thought, sentiment, imagination, and soul, in respect to every element except that of place of physical being—a thing that means so much to some—is as universal as any personality in literature. That he said upon being shown a specimen grass from Iceland that the same species could be found in Concord is evidence of his universality, not of his parochialism. He was so universal that he did not need to travel around the world to *prove* it. "I have more of God, they more of the road." "It is not worth while to go around the world to count the cats in Zanzibar." With Marcus Aurelius, if he had seen the present he had seen all, from eternity and all time forever.

Thoreau's susceptibility to natural sounds was probably greater than that of many practical musicians. True, this appeal is mainly through the sensational element which Herbert Spencer thinks the predominant beauty of music. Thoreau seems able to weave from this source some perfect transcendental symphonies. Strains from the Orient get the best of some of the modern French music but not of Thoreau. He seems more interested *in* than influenced *by* Oriental philosophy. He admires its ways of resignation and self-contemplation but he doesn't contemplate himself in the same way. He often quotes from the Eastern scriptures passages which were they his own he would probably omit, *i.e.*, the Vedas say "all intelligences awake with the morning." This seems unworthy of "accompanying the undulations of celestial music" found on this same page, in which an "ode to morning" is sung—"the awakening to newly acquired forces and aspirations from within to a higher life than we fell asleep from . . . for *all* memorable events transpire in the morning time and in the morning atmosphere." Thus it is not the whole tone scale of the Orient but the scale of a Walden morning—"music in single strains," as Emerson says, which inspired many of the polyphonies and harmonies that come to us through his poetry. Who can be forever melancholy "with Æolian music like this"?

This is but one of many ways in which Thoreau looked to Nature for his greatest inspirations. In her he found an analogy to the Fundamental of Transcendentalism. The "innate goodness" of Nature is or can be a moral influence; Mother Nature, if man will but let her, will keep him straight—straight spiritually and so morally and even mentally. If he will take her as a companion, and teacher, and *not* as a duty or a creed, she will give him greater thrills and teach him greater truths than man can give or teach—she will reveal mysteries that mankind has long concealed. It was the soul of Nature not natural history that Thoreau was after. A naturalist's mind is one predominantly scientific, more interested in the relation of a flower to other flowers than its relation to any philosophy or anyone's philosophy. A transcendent love of Nature and writing "Rhus glabra" after sumach doesn't necessarily make a naturalist. It would seem that although thorough in observation (not very thorough according to Mr. Burroughs) and with a keen perception of the specific, a naturalist—inherently—was exactly what Thoreau was *not*. He seems rather to let Nature put him under her microscope than to hold her under his. He was too fond of Nature to practice vivisection upon her. He would have found that painful, "for was he not a part with her?" But he had this trait of a naturalist, which is usually foreign to poets, even great ones; he observed acutely even things that did not particularly interest him—a useful natural gift rather than a virtue.

The study of Nature may tend to make one dogmatic, but the love of Nature surely does not. Thoreau no more than Emerson could be said to have compounded doctrines. His thinking was too broad for that. If Thoreau's was a religion of Nature, as some say,—and by that they mean that through Nature's influence man is brought to a deeper contemplation, to a more spiritual self-scrutiny, and thus closer to God,—it had apparently no definite doctrines. Some of his theories regarding natural and social phenomena and his experiments in the art of living are certainly not doctrinal in form, and if they are in substance it didn't disturb Thoreau and it needn't us. . . . "In proportion as he simplifies his life the laws of the universe will appear less complex and solitude will not be solitude, nor poverty poverty, nor weakness weakness. If you have built castles in the air your work need not be lost; that is where they should be, now put the foundations under them." . . . "Then we will love with the license of a higher order of beings." Is that a doctrine? Perhaps. At any rate, between the lines of some such passage as this lie some of the fountain heads that water the spiritual fields of his philosophy and the seeds from which they are sown (if indeed his whole philosophy is but one spiritual garden). His experiments, social and economic, are a part of its cultivation and for the harvest—and its transmutation, he trusts to moments of inspiration—"only what is thought, said, and done at a certain rare coincidence is good."

Thoreau's experiment at Walden was, broadly speaking, one of these moments. It stands out in the casual and popular opinion as a kind of adventure—harmless and amusing to some, significant and important to others; but its significance lies in the fact that in trying to practice an ideal he prepared his mind so that it could better bring others "into the Walden-state-of-mind." He did not ask for a literal approval, or in fact for any approval. "I would not stand between any man and his genius." He would have no one adopt his manner of life, unless in doing so he adopts his own—besides, by that time "I may have found a better one." But if he preached hard he practiced harder what he preached—harder than most men. Throughout Walden a text that he is always pounding out is "Time." Time for inside work out-of-doors; preferably out-of-doors, "though you perhaps may have some pleasant, thrilling, glorious hours, even in a poor house." Wherever the place—time there must be. Time to show the unnecessariness of necessities which clog up time. Time to contemplate the value of man to the universe, of the universe to man, man's excuse for being. Time *from* the demands of social conventions. Time *from* too much labor for some, which means too much to eat, too much to wear, too much material, too much materialism for others. Time *from* the "hurry and waste of life." Time *from* the "St. Vitus Dance." *But,* on the other side of the ledger, time *for* learning that "there is no safety in stupidity alone." Time *for* introspection. Time *for* reality. Time *for* expansion. Time *for* practicing the art, of living the art of living. Thoreau has been criticized for practicing his policy of expansion by living in a vacuum—but he peopled that vacuum with a race of beings and established a social order there, surpassing any of the precepts in social or political history. " . . . for he put some things behind and passed an invisible boundary; new, universal, and more liberal laws were around and within him, the old laws were expanded and interpreted in a more liberal sense and he lived with the license of a higher order"—a community in which "God was the only President" and "Thoreau not Webster was His Orator." It is hard to believe that Thoreau really refused to believe that there was any other life but his own, though he probably did think that there was not any other life besides his own for him. Living for society may not always be best accomplished by living *with* society. "Is there any virtue in a man's skin that you must touch it?" and the "rubbing of elbows may not bring men's minds closer together"; or if he were talking through a "worst seller" (magazine) that "had to put it over" he might say, "forty thousand souls at a ball game does not, necessarily, make baseball the highest expression of spiritual emotion." Thoreau, however, is no cynic, either in character or thought, though in a side glance at himself, he may have held out to be one; a "cynic in independence," possibly because of his rule laid down that "self-culture admits of no compromise."

It is conceivable that though some of his philosophy and a good deal of his personality, in some of its manifestations, have outward colors that do not seem to harmonize, the true and intimate relations they bear each other are not affected. This peculiarity, frequently seen in his attitude towards social-economic problems, is perhaps more emphasized in some of his personal outbursts. "I love my friends very much, but I find that it is of no use to go to see them. I hate them commonly when I am near." It is easier to see what he means than it is to forgive him for saying it. The cause of this apparent lack of harmony between philosophy and personality, as far as they can be separated, may have been due to his refusal "to keep the very delicate balance" which Mr. Van Doren in his *Critical Study of Thoreau* says "it is necessary for a great and good man to keep between his public and private lives, between his own personality and the whole outside universe of personalities." Somehow one feels that if he had kept this balance he would have lost "hitting power." Again, it seems that something of the above depends upon the degree of greatness or goodness. A very great and especially a very good man has no separate private and public life. His own personality though not identical with outside personalities is so clear or can be so clear to them that it appears identical, and as the world progresses towards its inevitable perfection this appearance becomes more and more a reality. For the same reason that all great men now agree, in principle but not in detail, in so far as words are able to communicate agreement, on the great fundamental truths. Someone says: "Be specific—what great fundamentals?" Freedom over slavery; the natural over the artificial; beauty over ugliness; the spiritual over the material; the goodness of man; the Godness of man;

God; with all other kindred truths that have been growing in expression through the ages, eras, and civilizations, innate things which once seemed foreign to the soul of humankind. All great men—there are millions of them now—agree on these. Around the relative and the absolute value of an attribute, or quality, or whatever it may be called, is where the fight is. The relative not *from* the absolute—but *of* it, always *of* it. Geniuses—and there are millions of them—differ as to *what* is beautiful and *what* is ugly, as to *what* is right and *what* is wrong—there are many interpretations of God—but they all agree that beauty is better than ugliness and right is better than wrong, and that there is a God—all are one when they reach the essence. Every analysis of a criticism or quality of Thoreau invariably leads back and stands us against the great problems of life and eternity. It is a fair indication of the greatness of his problems and ideals.

The unsympathetic treatment accorded Thoreau on account of the false colors that his personality apparently gave to some of his important ideas and virtues, might be lessened if it were more constantly remembered that a command of his to-day is but a mood of yesterday and a contradiction to-morrow. He is too volatile to paint, much less to catalogue. If Thoreau did not over-say he said nothing. He says so himself. "I desire to speak somewhere without bounds like a man in a waking moment to men in their waking moments . . . for I am convinced that I cannot exaggerate enough even to lay a foundation for a true expression." For all that, it is not safe to think that he should *never* be taken literally, as for instance in the sentence above. His extravagance at times involves him but Thoreau never rejoices in it as Meredith seems to. He struggles against it and seems as much ashamed of being involved as the latter seems of not being. He seldom gets into the situation of Meredith—timidly wandering around with no clothes after stepping out of one of his involvedensities. This habit may be a part of the novelists' license, for perhaps their inspiration is less original and less natural than that of the poets, as traits of human weakness are unnatural to or "not an innate part with human nature." Perhaps if they (novelists) had broader sources for their inspiration they would hardly need licenses and perhaps they would hardly become novelists. For the same reason that Shakespeare might have been greater if he hadn't written plays. Some say that a true composer will never write an opera because a truly brave man will not take a drink to keep up his courage; which is not the same thing as saying that Shakespeare is not the greatest figure in all literature; in fact, it is an attempt to say that many novels, most operas, all Shakespeares, and all brave men and women (rum or no rum) are among the noblest blessings with which God has endowed mankind—because, not being perfect, they are perfect examples pointing to that perfection which nothing yet has attained.

Thoreau's mysticism at times throws him into elusive moods —but an elusiveness held by a thread to something concrete and specific, for he had too much integrity of mind for any other kind. In these moments it is easier to follow his thought than to follow him. Indeed, if he were always easy to follow, after one had caught up with him, one might find that it was not Thoreau.

It is, however, with no mystic rod that he strikes at institutional life. Here again he felt the influence of the great transcendental doctrine of "innate goodness" in human nature—a reflection of the like in nature; a philosophic part which, by the way, was a more direct inheritance in Thoreau than in his brother transcendentalists. For besides what he received from a native Unitarianism a good part must have descended to him through his Huguenot blood from the "eighteenth-century French philosophy." We trace a reason here for his lack of interest in "the church." For if revealed religion is the path between God and man's spiritual part—a kind of formal causeway —Thoreau's highly developed spiritual life felt, apparently unconsciously, less need of it than most men. But he might have been more charitable towards those who do need it (and most of·us do) if he had been·more conscious of his freedom. Those who look to-day for the cause of a seeming deterioration in the influence of the church may find it in a wider development of this feeling of Thoreau's; that the need is less because there is more of the spirit of Christianity in the world to-day. Another cause for his attitude towards the church as an institution is one always too common among "the narrow minds" to have influenced Thoreau. He could have been more generous. He took the arc for the circle, the exception for the rule, the solitary bad example for the many good ones. His persistent emphasis on the value of "example" may excuse this lower viewpoint. "The silent influence of the example of one sincere life . . . has benefited society more than all the projects devised for its salvation." He has little patience for the unpracticing preacher. "In some countries a hunting parson is no uncommon sight. Such a one might make a good shepherd dog but is far from being a good shepherd." It would have been interesting to have seen him handle the speculating parson, who takes a good salary—more per annum than all the disciples had to sustain their bodies during their whole lives—from a metropolitan religious corporation for "speculating" on Sunday about the beauty of poverty, who preaches: "Take no thought (for your life) what ye shall eat or what ye shall drink nor yet what ye shall put on . . . lay not up for yourself treasure upon earth . . . take up thy cross and follow me"; who on Monday becomes a "speculating" disciple of another god, and by questionable investments, successful enough to get into the "press," seeks to lay up a treasure of a million dollars for his old age, as if a million dollars could keep such a man out of the poor-house. Thoreau might observe that this one good example of Christian degeneracy undoes all the acts of regeneracy of a thousand humble five-hundred-dollar country parsons; that it out-influences the "unconscious influence" of a dozen Dr. Bushnells if there be that many; that the repentance of this man who did not "fall from grace" because he never fell into it—that this unnecessary repentance might save this man's own soul but not necessarily the souls of the million head-line readers; that repentance would put this preacher right with the powers that be in this world—and the next. Thoreau might pass a remark upon this man's intimacy with God "as if he had a monopoly of the subject"—an intimacy that perhaps kept him from asking God exactly what his Son meant by the "camel," the "needle"—to say nothing of the "rich man." Thoreau might have wondered how this man *nailed down* the last plank in *his* bridge to salvation, by rising to sublime heights of patriotism, in *his* war against materialism; but would even Thoreau be so unfeeling as to suggest to this exhorter that *his* salvation might be clinched "if he would sacrifice his income" (not himself) and come-in to a real Salvation Army, or that the final triumph, the supreme happiness in casting aside this mere $10,000 or $20,000 every year must be denied him—for was he not captain of the ship—must he not stick to his passengers (in the first cabin—the very first cabin)—not that the *ship* was sinking but that *he* was . . . we will go no further. Even Thoreau would not demand sacrifice for sacrifice sake—no, not even from Nature.

Property from the standpoint of its influence in checking natural self-expansion and from the standpoint of personal and inherent right is another institution that comes in for straight and cross-arm jabs, now to the stomach, now to the head, but seldom sparring for breath. For does he not say that "wherever a man goes, men will pursue him with their dirty institutions"? The influence of property, as he saw it, on morality or immorality and how through this it may or should influence "government" is seen by the following: "I am convinced that if all men were to live as simply as I did, then thieving and robbery would be unknown. These take place only in communities where some have got more than is sufficient while others have not enough—

> Nec bella fuerunt,
> Faginus astabat dum
> Scyphus ante dapes—

You who govern public affairs, what need have you to employ punishments? Have virtue and the people will be virtuous." If Thoreau had made the first sentence read: "If all men were *like* me and were to live as simply," etc., everyone would agree with him. We may wonder here how he would account for some of the degenerate types we are told about in some of our backwoods and mountain regions. Possibly by assuming that they are an instance of perversion of the species. That the little civilizing their forbears experienced rendered these people more susceptible to the physical than to the spiritual influence of nature; in other words, if they had been purer naturists, as the Aztecs for example, they would have been purer men. Instead of turning to any theory of ours or of Thoreau for the true explanation of this condition—which is a kind of pseudo-naturalism—for its true diagnosis and permanent cure, are we not far more certain to find it in the radiant look of humility, love, and hope in the strong faces of those inspired souls who are devoting their lives with no little sacrifice to these outcasts of civilization and nature. In truth, may not mankind find the solution of its eternal problem—find it after and beyond the last, most perfect system of wealth distribution which science can ever devise—after and beyond the last sublime echo of the greatest socialistic symphonies—after and beyond every transcendent thought and expression in the simple example of these Christ-inspired souls—be they Pagan, Gentile, Jew, or angel.

However, underlying the practical or impractical suggestions implied in the quotation above, which is from the last paragraph of Thoreau's *Village*, is the same transcendental theme of "innate goodness." For this reason there must be no limitation except that which will free mankind from limitation, and from a perversion of this "innate" possession. And "property" may be one of the causes of this perversion—property in the two relations cited above. It is conceivable that Thoreau, to the consternation of the richest members of the Bolsheviki and Bourgeois, would propose a policy of liberation, a policy of a limited personal property right, on the ground that congestion of personal property tends to limit the progress of the soul (as well as the progress of the stomach)—letting the economic noise thereupon take care of itself—for dissonances are becoming beautiful—and do not the same waters that roar in a storm take care of the eventual calm? That this limit of property be determined not by the *voice* of the majority but by the *brain* of the majority under a government limited to no national boundaries. "The government of the world I live in is not framed in after-dinner conversation"—around a table in a capital city, for there is no capital—a government of principles not parties; of a few fundamental truths and not of many political expediencies. A government conducted by virtuous leaders, for it will be led by all, for all are virtuous, as then their "innate virtue" will no more be perverted by unnatural institutions. This will not be a millennium but a practical and possible application of uncommon common sense. For is it not sense, common or otherwise, for Nature to want to hand back the earth to those to whom it belongs—that is, to those who have to live on it? Is it not sense, that the average brains like the average stomachs will act rightly if they have an equal amount of the right kind of food to act upon and universal education is on the way with the right kind of food? Is it not sense then that all grown men and women (for *all* are necessary to work out the divine "law of averages") shall have a *direct* not an *indirect* say about the things that go on in this world?

Some of these attitudes, ungenerous or radical, generous or conservative (as you will), towards institutions dear to many, have no doubt given impressions unfavorable to Thoreau's thought and personality. One hears him called, by some who ought to know what they say and some who ought not, a crabbed, cold-hearted, sour-faced Yankee—a kind of a visionary sore-head —a cross-grained, egotistic recluse,—even non-hearted. But it is easier to make a statement than prove a reputation. Thoreau may be some of these things to those who make no distinction between these qualities and the manner which often comes as a kind of by-product of an intense devotion of a principle or ideal. He was rude and unfriendly at times but shyness probably had something to do with that. In spite of a certain self-possession he was diffident in most company, but, though he may have been subject to those spells when words do not rise and the mind seems wrapped in a kind of dull cloth which everyone dumbly stares at, instead of looking through—he would easily get off a rejoinder upon occasion. When a party of visitors came to Walden and some one asked Thoreau if he found it lonely there, he replied: "Only by your help." A remark characteristic, true, rude, if not witty. The writer remembers hearing a schoolteacher in English literature dismiss Thoreau (and a half hour lesson, in which time all of Walden,—its surface—was sailed over) by saying that this author (he called everyone "author" from Solomon down to Dr. Parkhurst) "was a kind of a crank who styled himself a hermit-naturalist and who idled about the woods because he didn't want to work." Some such stuff is a common conception, though not as common as it used to be. If this teacher had had more brains, it would have been a lie. The word *idled* is the hopeless part of this criticism, or rather of this uncritical remark. To ask this kind of a man, who plays all the "choice gems from celebrated composers" literally, always literally, and always with the loud pedal, who plays all hymns, wrong notes, right notes, games, people, and jokes literally, and with the loud pedal, who will die literally and with the loud pedal—to ask this man to smile even faintly at Thoreau's humor is like casting a pearl before a coal baron. Emerson implies that there is one thing a genius must have to be a *genius* and that is "mother wit." . . . "Doctor Johnson, Milton, Chaucer, and Burns had it. Aunt Mary Moody Emerson has it and can write scrap letters. Who has it need never write anything but scraps. Henry Thoreau has it." His humor though a part of this wit is not always as spontaneous, for it is sometimes pun shape (so is Charles Lamb's)—but it is nevertheless a kind that can serenely transport us and which we can enjoy without disturbing our neighbors. If there are those who think him cold-hearted and with but little human sympathy, let them read his letters to Emerson's little daughter, or hear Dr. Emerson tell about the Thoreau home life and the stories of his boyhood—the ministrations to a runaway slave; or let them ask old Sam Staples, the Concord sheriff about him. That he "was fond of a few intimate friends, but cared not one fig for people in the mass," is a statement made in a school history and which is superficially true. He cared too much for the masses—too much to let his personality be "massed"; too much to be unable to realize the futility of wearing his heart on his sleeve but not of wearing his path to the shore of "Walden" for future masses to walk over and perchance find the way to themselves. Some near-satirists are fond of telling us that Thoreau came so close to Nature that she killed him before he had discovered her whole secret. They remind us that he died with consumption but forget that he lived with consumption. And without using much charity, this can be made to excuse many of his irascible and uncongenial moods. You to whom that gaunt face seems forbidding—look into the eyes! If he seems "dry and priggish" to you, Mr. Stevenson, "with little of that large unconscious geniality of the world's heroes," follow him some spring morning to Baker Farm, as he "rambles through pine groves . . . like temples, or like fleets at sea, full-rigged, with wavy boughs and rippling with light so soft and green and shady that the Druids would have forsaken their oaks to worship in them." Follow him to "the cedar wood beyond

Flint's Pond, where the trees covered with hoary blue berries, spiring higher and higher, are fit to stand before Valhalla." Follow him, but not too closely, for you may see little, if you do—"as he walks in so pure and bright a light gilding its withered grass and leaves so softly and serenely bright that he thinks he has never bathed in such a golden flood." Follow him as "he saunters towards the holy land till one day the sun shall shine more brightly than ever it has done, perchance shine into your minds and hearts and light up your whole lives with a great awakening, light as warm and serene and golden as on a bankside in autumn." Follow him through the golden flood to the shore of that "holy land," where he lies dying as men say—dying as bravely as he lived. You may be near when his stern old aunt in the duty of her Puritan conscience asks him: "Have you made your peace with God"? and you may see his kindly smile as he replies, "I did not know that we had ever quarreled." Moments like these reflect more nobility and equanimity perhaps than geniality—qualities, however, more serviceable to world's heroes.

The personal trait that one who has affection for Thoreau may find worst is a combative streak, in which he too often takes refuge. "An obstinate elusiveness," almost a "contrary cussed-ness," as if he would say, which he didn't: "If a truth about something is not as I think it ought to be, I'll make it what I think, and it *will* be the truth—but if you agree with me, then I begin to think it may not be the truth." The causes of these unpleasant colors (rather than characteristics) are too easily attributed to a lack of human sympathy or to the assumption that they are at least symbols of that lack instead of to a super-sensitiveness, magnified at times by ill health and at times by a subconsciousness of the futility of actually living out his ideals in this life. It has been said that his brave hopes were unrealized anywhere in his career—but it is certain that they started to be realized on or about May 6, 1862, and we doubt if 1920 will end their fulfillment or his career. But there were many in Concord who knew that within their village there was a tree of wondrous growth, the shadow of which—alas, too frequently—was the only part they were allowed to touch. Emerson was one of these. He was not only deeply conscious of Thoreau's rare gifts but in the

Woodland Notes pays a tribute to a side of his friend that many others missed. Emerson knew that Thoreau's sensibilities too often veiled his nobilities, that a self-cultivated stoicism ever fortified with sarcasm, none the less securely because it seemed voluntary, covered a warmth of feeling. "His great heart, him a hermit made." A breadth of heart not easily measured, found only in the highest type of sentimentalists, the type which does not perpetually discriminate in favor of mankind. Emerson has much of this sentiment and touches it when he sings of Nature as "the incarnation of a thought," when he generously visualizes Thoreau, "standing at the Walden shore invoking the vision of a thought as it drifts heavenward into an incarnation of Nature." There is a Godlike patience in Nature,—in her mists, her trees, her mountains—as if she had a more abiding faith and a clearer vision than man of the resurrection and immortality!

There comes to memory an old yellow-papered composition of school-boy days whose peroration closed with "Poor Thoreau; he communed with nature for forty odd years, and then died." "The forty odd years,"—we'll still grant that part, but he is over a hundred now, and maybe, Mr. Lowell, he is more lovable, kindlier, and more radiant with human sympathy to-day, than, perchance, you were fifty years ago. It may be that he is a far stronger, a far greater, an incalculably greater force in the moral and spiritual fibre of his fellow-countrymen throughout the world to-day than you dreamed of fifty years ago. You, James Russell Lowells! You, Robert Louis Stevensons! You, Mark Van Dorens! with your literary perception, your power of illumination, your brilliancy of expression, yea, and with your love of sincerity, you know your Thoreau, but not my Thoreau—that reassuring and true friend, who stood by me one "low" day, when the sun had gone down, long, long before sunset. You may know something of the affection that heart yearned for but knew it a duty not to grasp; you may know something of the great human passions which stirred that soul—too deep for animate expression—you may know all of this, all there is to know about Thoreau, but you know him not, unless you love him!

And if there shall be a program for our music let it follow his thought on an autumn day of Indian summer at Walden—

a shadow of a thought at first, colored by the mist and haze over the pond:

> Low anchored cloud,
> Fountain head and
> Source of rivers. . . .
> Dew cloth, dream drapery—
> Drifting meadow of the air. . . .

but this is momentary; the beauty of the day moves him to a certain restlessness—to aspirations more specific—an eagerness for outward action, but through it all he is conscious that it is not in keeping with the mood for this "Day." As the mists rise, there comes a clearer thought more traditional than the first, a meditation more calm. As he stands on the side of the pleasant hill of pines and hickories in front of his cabin, he is still disturbed by a restlessness and goes down the white-pebbled and sandy eastern shore, but it seems not to lead him where the thought suggests— he climbs the path along the "bolder northern" and "western shore, with deep bays indented," and now along the railroad track, "where the Æolian harp plays." But his eagerness throws him into the lithe, springy stride of the specie hunter—the naturalist—he is still aware of a restlessness; with these faster steps his rhythm is of shorter span—it is still not the *tempo* of Nature, it does not bear the mood that the genius of the day calls for, it is too specific, its nature is too external, the introspection too buoyant, and he knows now that he must let Nature flow through *him* and slowly; he releases his more personal desires to her broader rhythm, conscious that this blends more and more with the harmony of her solitude; it tells him that his search for freedom on that day, at least, lies in his submission to her, for Nature is as relentless as she is benignant. He remains in this mood and while outwardly still, he seems to move with the slow, almost monotonous swaying beat of this autumnal day. He is more contented with a "homely burden" and is more assured of "the broad margin to his life; he sits in his sunny doorway . . . rapt in revery . . . amidst goldenrod, sandcherry, and sumach . . . in undisturbed solitude." At times the more definite personal strivings for the ideal freedom, the former more active speculations come over him, as if he would trace a certain intensity even in his submission. "He grew in those seasons like corn in the night and they were better than any works of the hands. They were not time subtracted from his life but so much over and above the usual allowance." "He realized what the Orientals meant by contemplation and forsaking of works." "The day advanced as if to light some work of his—it was morning and lo! now it is evening and nothing memorable is accomplished . . ." "The evening train has gone by," and "all the restless world with it. The fishes in the pond no longer feel its rumbling and he is more alone than ever. . . ." His meditations are interrupted only by the faint sound of the Concord bell—'tis prayer-meeting night in the village—"a melody as it were, imported into the wilderness. . . ." "At a distance over the woods the sound acquires a certain vibratory hum as if the pine needles in the horizon were the strings of a harp which it swept. . . . A vibration of the universal lyre. . . . Just as the intervening atmosphere makes a distant ridge of earth interesting to the eyes by the azure tint it imparts." . . . Part of the echo may be "the voice of the wood; the same trivial words and notes sung by the wood nymph." It is darker, the poet's flute is heard out over the pond and Walden hears the swan song of that "Day" and faintly echoes. . . . Is it a transcendental tune of Concord? 'Tis an evening when the "whole body is one sense," . . . and before ending his day he looks out over the clear, crystalline water of the pond and catches a glimpse of the shadow-thought he saw in the morning's mist and haze—he knows that by his final submission, he possesses the "Freedom of the Night." He goes up the "pleasant hillside of pines, hickories," and moonlight to his cabin, "with a strange liberty in Nature, a part of herself."

VI Epilogue

1

The futility of attempting to trace the source or primal impulse of an art-inspiration may be admitted without granting that human qualities or attributes which go with personality cannot be suggested, and that artistic intuitions which parallel them cannot be reflected in music. Actually accomplishing the latter is a problem, more or less arbitrary to an open mind, more or less impossible to a prejudiced mind.

That which the composer intends to represent as "high vitality" sounds like something quite different to different listeners. That which I like to think suggests Thoreau's submission to nature may, to another, seem something like Hawthorne's "conception of the relentlessness of an evil conscience"—and to the rest of our friends, but a series of unpleasant sounds. How far can the composer be held accountable? Beyond a certain point the responsibility is more or less undeterminable. The outside characteristics—that is, the points furthest away from the mergings—are obvious to mostly anyone. A child knows a "strain of joy," from one of sorrow. Those a little older know the dignified from the frivolous—the Spring Song from the season in which the "melancholy days have come" (though is there not a glorious hope in autumn!). But where is the definite expression of late-spring against early-summer, of happiness against optimism? A painter paints a sunset—can he paint the setting sun?

In some century to come, when the school children will whistle popular tunes in quarter-tones—when the diatonic scale will be as obsolete as the pentatonic is now—perhaps then these borderland experiences may be both easily expressed and readily recognized. But maybe music was not intended to satisfy the curious definiteness of man. Maybe it is better to hope that music may always be a transcendental language in the most extravagant sense. Possibly the power of literally distinguishing these "shades of abstraction"—these attributes paralleled by "artistic intuitions" (call them what you will)—is ever to be denied man for the same reason that the beginning and end of a circle are to be denied.

2

There may be an analogy—and on first sight it seems that there must be—between both the state and power of artistic perceptions and the law of perpetual change, that ever-flowing stream partly biological, partly cosmic, ever going on in ourselves, in nature, in all life. This may account for the difficulty of identifying desired qualities with the perceptions of them in expression. Many things are constantly coming into being, while others are constantly going out—one part of the same thing is coming in while another part is going out of existence. Perhaps this is why the above conformity in art (a conformity which we seem naturally to look for) appears at times so unrealizable, if not impossible. It will be assumed, to make this theory clearer, that the "flow" or "change" does not go on in the art-product itself. As a matter of fact it probably does, to a certain extent— a picture, or a song, may gain or lose in value beyond what the painter or composer knew, by the progress and higher development in all art. Keats may be only partially true when he says that "A work of beauty is a joy forever"—a thing that is beautiful *to me*, is a joy *to me*, as long as it remains beautiful *to me*— and if it remains so as long as I live, it is so forever, that is, forever *to me*. If he had put it this way, he would have been tiresome, inartistic, but perhaps truer. So we will assume here that this change only goes on in man and nature; and that this eternal process in mankind is paralleled in some way during each temporary, personal life.

A young man, two generations ago, found an identity with his ideals, in Rossini; when an older man in Wagner. A young man, one generation ago, found his in Wagner, but when older in César Franck or Brahms. Some may say that this change may not be general, universal, or natural, and that it may be due to a certain kind of education, or to a certain inherited or contracted prejudice. We cannot deny or affirm this, absolutely, nor will we try to even qualitatively—except to say that it will be generally admitted that Rossini, to-day, does not appeal to this generation, as he did to that of our fathers. As far as prejudice or undue influence is concerned, and as an illustration in point, the following may be cited to show that training may have but little effect in this connection, at least not as much as usually supposed—for we believe this experience to be, to a certain extent, normal, or at least, not uncommon. A man remembers, when he was a boy of about fifteen years, hearing his music-teacher (and father) who had just returned from a performance of *Siegfried* say with a look of anxious surprise that "somehow or other he felt ashamed of enjoying the music as he did," for beneath it all he was conscious of an undercurrent of "make-believe"—the bravery was make-believe, the love was make-believe, the passion, the virtue, all make-believe, as was the dragon —P. T. Barnum would have been brave enough to have gone out and captured a live one! But, that same boy at twenty-five was listening to Wagner with enthusiasm, his reality was real enough to inspire a devotion. The "Preis-Lied," for instance, stirred him deeply. But when he became middle-aged—and long before the Hohenzollern hog-marched into Belgium—this music had become cloying, the melodies threadbare—a sense of something commonplace—yes—of make-believe came. These feelings were fought against for association's sake, and because of gratitude for bygone pleasures—but the former beauty and nobility were not there, and in their place stood irritating intervals of descending fourths and fifths. Those once transcendent progressions, luxuriant suggestions of Debussy chords of the 9th, 11th, etc., were becoming slimy. An unearned exultation—a sentimentality deadening something within hides around in the music. Wagner seems less and less to measure up to the substance and reality of César Franck, Brahms, d'Indy, or even Elgar (with all his tiresomeness), the wholesomeness, manliness, humility, and deep spiritual, possibly religious feeling of these men seem missing and not made up for by his (Wagner's) manner and eloquence, even if greater than theirs (which is very doubtful).

From the above we would try to prove that as this stream of change flows towards the eventual ocean of mankind's perfection, the art-works in which we identify our higher ideals come by this process to be identified with the lower ideals of those who embark after us when the stream has grown in depth. If we stop with the above experience, our theory of the effect of man's changing nature, as thus explaining artistic progress, is perhaps sustained. Thus would we show that the perpetual flow of the life stream is affected by and affects each individual river-bed of the universal watersheds. Thus would we prove that the Wagner period was normal, because we intuitively recognized whatever identity we were looking for at a certain period in our life, and the fact that it was so made the Franck period possible and then normal at a later period in our life. Thus would we assume that this is as it should be, and that it is not Wagner's content or substance or his lack of virtue, that something in us has made us flow past him and not he past us. But something blocks our theory! Something makes our hypotheses seem purely speculative if not useless. It is men like Bach and Beethoven.

Is it not a matter nowadays of common impression or general opinion (for the law of averages plays strongly in any theory relating to human attributes) that the world's attitude towards the substance and quality and spirit of these two men, or other men of like character, if there be such, has not been affected by the flowing stream that has changed us? But if by the measure of this public opinion, as well as it can be measured, Bach and Beethoven are being flowed past—not as fast perhaps as Wagner is, but if they are being passed at all from this deeper viewpoint, then this "change" theory holds.

Here we shall have to assume, for we haven't proved it, that artistic intuitions can sense in music a weakening of moral strength and vitality, and that it is sensed in relation to Wagner and not sensed in relation to Bach and Beethoven. If, in this common opinion, there is a particle of change toward the latter's art, our theory stands—mind you, this admits a change in the manner, form, external expression, etc., but not in substance. If there is no change here towards the substance of these two men, our theory not only falls but its failure superimposes or allows us to presume a fundamental duality in music, and in all art for that matter.

Does the progress of intrinsic beauty or truth (we assume there is such a thing) have its exposures as well as its discoveries? Does the non-acceptance of the foregoing theory mean that Wagner's substance and reality are lower and his manner higher; that his beauty was not intrinsic; that he was more interested in the repose of pride than in the truth of humility? It appears that he chose the representative instead of the spirit itself,—that he chose consciously or unconsciously, it matters not,—the lower set of values in this dualism. These are severe accusations to bring—especially when a man is a little down as Wagner is to-day. But these convictions were present some time before he was banished from the Metropolitan.

Wagner seems to take Hugo's place in Faguet's criticism of de Vigny that, "The staging to him (Hugo) was the important thing—not the conception—that in de Vigny, the artist was inferior to the poet"; finally that Hugo and so Wagner have a certain *pauvreté de fond*. Thus would we ungenerously make Wagner prove our sum! But it is a sum that won't prove! The theory at its best does little more than suggest something, which if it is true at all, is a platitude, viz.: that progressive growth in all life makes it more and more possible for men to separate, in an art-work, moral weakness from artistic strength.

3

Human attributes are definite enough when it comes to their description, but the expression of them, or the paralleling of them in an art-process, has to be, as said above, more or less arbitrary, but we believe that their expression can be less vague if the basic distinction of this art-dualism is kept in mind. It is morally certain that the higher part is founded, as Sturt suggests, on something that has to do with those kinds of unselfish human interests which we call knowledge and morality—knowledge, not in the sense of erudition, but as a kind of creation or creative truth. This allows us to assume that the higher and more important value of this dualism is composed of what may be called reality, quality, spirit, or substance against the lower value of form, quantity, or manner. Of these terms "substance" seems to us the most appropriate, cogent, and comprehensive for the higher and "manner" for the under-value. Substance in a human-art-quality suggests the body of a conviction which has its birth in the spiritual consciousness, whose youth is nourished in the moral consciousness, and whose maturity as a result of all this growth is then represented in a mental image. This is appreciated by the intuition, and somehow translated into expression by "manner"—a process always less important than it seems, or as suggested by the foregoing (in fact we apologize for this attempted definition). So it seems that "substance" is too indefinite to analyze, in more specific terms. It is practically indescribable. Intuitions (artistic or not?) will sense it—process, unknown. Perhaps it is an unexplained consciousness of being nearer God, or being nearer the devil—of approaching truth or approaching unreality—a silent something felt in the truth-of-nature in Turner against the truth-of-art in Botticelli, or in the fine thinking of Ruskin against the fine soundings of Kipling, or in the wide-expanse of Titian against the narrow-expanse of Carpaccio, or in some such distinction that Pope sees between what he calls Homer's ."invention" and Virgil's "judgment"—apparently an inspired imagination against an artistic care, a sense of the difference, perhaps, between Dr. Bushnell's *Knowing God* and knowing *about* God. A more vivid explanation or illustration may be found in the difference between Emerson and Poe. The former seems to be almost wholly "substance" and the latter "manner." The measure in artistic satisfaction of Poe's manner is equal to the measure of spiritual satisfaction in Emerson's "substance." The total value of each man is high, but Emerson's is higher than Poe's because "substance" is higher than "manner"—because "substance" leans towards optimism, and "manner" pessimism. We do not know that all this is so, but we feel, or rather know by intuition that it is so, in the same way we know intuitively that right is higher than wrong, though we can't always tell why a thing is right or wrong, or what is always the difference or the margin between right and wrong.

Beauty, in its common conception, has nothing to do with it (substance), unless it be granted that its outward aspect, or the expression between sensuous beauty and spiritual beauty can be always and distinctly known, which it cannot, as the art of music is still in its infancy. On reading this over, it seems only decent that some kind of an apology be made for the beginning of the preceding sentence. It cannot justly be said that anything that has to do with art has nothing to do with beauty in any degree,—that is, whether beauty is there or not, it has something to do with it. A casual idea of it, a kind of a first necessary-physical impression, was what we had in mind. Probably nobody knows what actual beauty is—except those serious writers of humorous essays in art magazines, who accurately, but kindly, with club in hand, demonstrate for all time and men that beauty is a quadratic monomial; that it *is* absolute; that it is relative; that it *is not* relative, that it *is not.* . . . The word "beauty" is as easy to use as the word "degenerate." Both come in handy when one does or does not agree with you. For our part, something that Roussel-Despierres says comes nearer to what we like to think beauty is . . . "an infinite source of good . . . the love of the beautiful . . . a constant anxiety for moral beauty." Even here we go around in a circle—a thing apparently inevitable, if one tries to reduce art to philosophy. But personally, we prefer to go around in a circle than around in a parallelepipedon, for it seems cleaner and perhaps freer from mathematics—or for the same reason we prefer Whittier to Baudelaire—a poet to a genius, or a healthy to a rotten apple—probably not so much because it is more nutritious, but because we like its taste better; we like the beautiful and don't like the ugly; therefore, what we like is beautiful, and what we don't like is ugly—and hence we are glad the beautiful is not ugly, for if it were we would like something we don't like. So having unsettled what beauty is, let us go on.

At any rate, we are going to be arbitrary enough to claim, with no definite qualification, that substance can be expressed in music, and that it is the only valuable thing in it, and moreover that in two separate pieces of music in which the notes are almost identical, one can be of "substance" with little "manner," and the other can be of "manner" with little "substance." Substance has something to do with character. Manner has nothing to do with it. The "substance" of a tune comes from somewhere near the soul, and the "manner" comes from—God knows where.

4

The lack of interest to preserve, or ability to perceive the fundamental divisions of this duality accounts to a large extent, we believe, for some or many various phenomena (pleasant or unpleasant according to the personal attitude) of modern art, and all art. It is evidenced in many ways—the sculptors' over-insistence on the "mold," the outer rather than the inner subject or content of his statue—over-enthusiasm for local color—over-interest in the multiplicity of techniques, in the idiomatic, in the effect as shown, by the appreciation of an audience rather than in the effect on the ideals of the inner conscience of the artist or the composer. This lack of perceiving is too often shown by an over-interest in the material value of the effect. The pose of self-absorption, which some men, in the advertising business (and incidentally in the recital and composing business) put into their photographs or the portraits of themselves, while all dolled up in their purple-dressing-gowns, in their twofold wealth of golden hair, in their cissy-like postures over the piano keys—this pose of "manner" sometimes sounds out so loud that the more their music is played, the less it is heard. For does not Emerson tell them this when he says "What you are talks so loud, that I cannot hear what you say"? The unescapable impression that one sometimes gets by a glance at these public-inflicted trade-marks, and without having heard or seen any of their music, is that the one great underlying desire of these appearing-artists, is to impress, perhaps startle and shock their audiences and at any cost. This may have some such effect upon some of the lady-part (male or female) of their listeners but possibly the members of the men-part, who as boys liked hockey better than birthday-parties, may feel like shocking a few of these picture-sitters with something stronger than their own forzandos.

The insistence upon manner in its relation to local color is wider than a self-strain for effect. If local color is a natural part, that is, a part of substance, the art-effort cannot help but show its color—and it will be a true color, no matter how colored; if it is a part, even a natural part of "manner," either the color part is bound eventually to drive out the local part or the local drive out all color. Here a process of cancellation or destruction is going on—a kind of "compromise" which destroys by deadlock; a compromise purchasing a selfish pleasure—a decadence in which art becomes first dull, then dark, then dead, though throughout this process it is outwardly very much alive,—especially after it is dead. The same tendency may even be noticed if there is over-insistence upon the national in art. Substance tends to create affection; manner prejudice. The latter tends to efface the distinction between the love of both a country's virtue and vices, and the love of only the virtue. A true love of country is likely to be so big that it will embrace the virtue one sees in other countries and, in the same breath, so to speak. A composer born in America, but who has not been interested in the "cause of the Freedmen," may be so interested in "negro melodies," that he writes a symphony over them. He is conscious (perhaps only subconscious) that he wishes it to be "American music." He tries to forget that the paternal negro came from Africa. Is his music American or African? That is the great question which keeps him awake! But the sadness of it is, that if he had been born in Africa, his music might have been just as American, for there is good authority that an African soul under an X-ray looks identically like an American soul. There is a futility in selecting a certain type to represent a "whole," unless the interest in the spirit of the type coincides with that of the whole. In other words, if this composer isn't as deeply interested in the "cause" as Wendell Phillips was, when he fought his way through that anti-abolitionist crowd at Faneuil Hall, his music is liable to be less American than he wishes. If a middle-aged man, upon picking up the *Scottish Chiefs*, finds that his boyhood enthusiasm for the prowess and noble deeds and character of Sir Wm. Wallace and of Bruce is still present, let him put, or try to put that glory into an overture, let him fill it chuck-full of Scotch tunes, if he will. But after all is said and sung he will find that his music is American to the core (assuming that he is an American and wishes his music to be). It will be as national in character as the heart of that Grand Army Grandfather, who read those *Cragmore Tales* of a summer evening, when that boy had brought the cows home without witching. Perhaps the memories of the old soldier, to which this man still holds tenderly, may be turned into a "strain" or a "sonata," and though the music does not contain, or even suggest any of the old war-songs, it will be as sincerely American as the subject, provided his (the composer's) interest, spirit, and character sympathize with, or intuitively coincide with that of the subject.

Again, if a man finds that the cadences of an Apache war-dance come nearest to his soul, provided he has taken pains to know enough other cadences—for eclecticism is part of his duty—sorting potatoes means a better crop next year—let him assimilate whatever he finds highest of the Indian ideal, so that he can use it with the cadences, fervently, transcendentally, inevitably, furiously, in his symphonies, in his operas, in his whistlings on the way to work, so that he can paint his house with them—make them a part of his prayer-book—this is all possible and necessary, if he is confident that they have a part in his spiritual consciousness. With this assurance his music will have everything it should of sincerity, nobility, strength, and beauty, no matter how it sounds; and if, with this, he is true to none but the highest of American ideals (that is, the ideals only that coincide with his spiritual consciousness) his music will be true to itself and incidentally American, and it will be so even after it is proved that all our Indians came from Asia.

The man "born down to Babbitt's Corners," may find a deep appeal in the simple but acute "Gospel Hymns of the New England camp meetin'," of a generation or so ago. He finds in them —some of them—a vigor, a depth of feeling, a natural-soil rhythm, a sincerity, emphatic but inartistic, which, in spite of a vociferous sentimentality, carries him nearer the "Christ of the people" than does the *Te Deum* of the greatest cathedral. These tunes have, for him, a truer ring than many of those groove-made, even-measured, monotonous, non-rhythmed, indoor-smelling, priest-taught, academic, English or neo-English hymns (and anthems) —well-written, well-harmonized things, well-voice-led, well-counterpointed, well corrected, and well O.K.'d, by well corrected Mus. Bac. R.F.O.G.'s—personified sounds, correct and inevitable to sight and hearing—in a word, those proper forms of stained-glass beauty, which our over-drilled mechanisms—boy-choirs are limited to. But, if the Yankee can reflect the fervency with which "his gospels" were sung—the fervency of "Aunt Sarah," who scrubbed her life away, for her brother's ten orphans, the fervency with which this woman, after a fourteen-hour work day on the farm, would hitch up and drive five miles, through the mud and rain to "prayer meetin' "—her one articulate outlet for the fullness of her unselfish soul—if he can reflect the fervency of such a spirit, he may find there a local color that will do all the world good. If his music can but catch that "spirit" by being a part with itself, it will come somewhere near his ideal—and it will be American, too, perhaps nearer so than that of the devotee of Indian or negro melody. In other words, if local color, national color, any color, is a true pigment of the universal color, it is a divine quality, it is a part of substance in art—not of manner.

The preceding illustrations are but attempts to show that whatever excellence an artist sees in life, a community, in a people, or in any valuable object or experience, if sincerely and intuitively reflected in his work, his work, and so he himself, is, in a way, a reflected part of that excellence. Whether he be accepted or rejected, whether his music is always played, or never played—all this has nothing to do with it—it is true or false by his own measure. If we may be permitted to leave out two words, and add a few more, a sentence of Hegel appears to sum up this idea, "The universal need for expression in art lies in man's rational impulse to exalt the inner . . . world (*i. e.,* the highest ideals he sees in the inner life of others) together with what he finds in his own life—into a spiritual consciousness for himself." The artist does feel or does not feel that a sympathy has been approved by an artistic intuition and so reflected in his work. Whether he feels this sympathy is true or not in the final analysis, is a thing probably that no one but he (the artist) knows— but the truer he feels it, the more substance it has, or as Sturt puts it, "his work *is* art, so long as he feels in doing it as true artists feel, and so long as his object is akin to the objects that true artists admire."

Dr. Griggs in an Essay on Debussy,[1] asks if this composer's content is worthy the manner. Perhaps so, perhaps not—Debussy himself, doubtless, could not give a positive answer. He would better know how true his feeling and sympathy was, and anyone else's personal opinion can be of but little help here.

We might offer the suggestion that Debussy's content would have been worthier his manner, if he had hoed corn or sold newspapers for a living, for in this way he might have gained a deeper vitality and truer theme to sing at night and of a Sunday. Or we might say that what substance there is, is "too coherent"—it is too clearly expressed in the first thirty seconds. There you have the "whole fragment," a translucent syllogism, but then the reality, the spirit, the substance stops and the "form," the "perfume," the "manner," shimmer right along, as the soapsuds glisten after one has finished washing. Or we might say that his substance would have been worthier, if his adoration or contemplation of Nature, which is often a part of it, and which rises to

[1] John C. Griggs, "Debussy," *Yale Review,* 1914.

great heights, as is felt for example, in *La Mer*, had been more the quality of Thoreau's. Debussy's attitude toward Nature seems to have a kind of sensual sensuousness underlying it, while Thoreau's is a kind of spiritual sensuousness. It is rare to find a farmer or peasant whose enthusiasm for the beauty in Nature finds outward expression to compare with that of the city-man who comes out for a Sunday in the country, but Thoreau is that rare country-man and Debussy the city-man with his week-end flights into country-æsthetics. We would be inclined to say that Thoreau leaned towards substance and Debussy towards manner.

5

There comes from Concord, an offer to every mind—the choice between repose and truth, and God makes the offer. "Take which you please . . . between these, as a pendulum, man oscillates. He in whom the love of repose predominates will accept the first creed, the first philosophy, the first political party he meets," most likely his father's. He gets rest, commodity, and reputation. Here is another aspect of art-duality, but it is more drastic than ours, as it would eliminate one part or the other. A man may aim as high as Beethoven or as high as Richard Strauss. In the former case the shot may go far below the mark; in truth, it has not been reached since that "thunder storm of 1828" and there is little chance that it will be reached by anyone living to-day, but that matters not, the shot will never rebound and destroy the marksman. But, in the latter case, the shot may often hit the mark, but as often rebound and harden, if not destroy, the shooter's heart—even his soul. What matters it, men say, he will then find rest, commodity, and reputation—what matters it —if he find there but few perfect truths—what matters (men say)—he will find there perfect media, those perfect instruments of getting in the way of perfect truths.

This choice tells why Beethoven is always modern and Strauss always mediæval—try as he may to cover it up in new bottles. He has chosen to capitalize a "talent"—he has chosen the complexity of media, the shining hardness of externals, repose, against the inner, invisible activity of truth. He has chosen the first creed, the easy creed, the philosophy of his fathers, among whom he found a half-idiot-genius (Nietzsche). His choice naturally leads him to glorify and to magnify all kind of dull things—a stretched-out *geigermusik*—which in turn naturally leads him to "windmills" and "human heads on silver platters." Magnifying the dull into the colossal, produces a kind of "comfort"—the comfort of a woman who takes more pleasure in the fit of fashionable clothes than in a healthy body—the kind of comfort that has brought so many "adventures of baby-carriages at county fairs"—"the sensation of Teddy bears, smoking their first cigarette"—on the program of symphony orchestras of one hundred performers,—the lure of the media—the means—not the end—but the finish,—thus the failure to perceive that thoughts and memories of childhood are too tender, and some of them too sacred to be worn lightly on the sleeve. Life is too short for these one hundred men, to say nothing of the composer and the "dress-circle," to spend an afternoon in this way. They are but like the rest of us, and have only the expectancy of the mortality-table to survive—perhaps only this "piece." We cannot but feel that a too great desire for "repose" accounts for such phenomena. A MS. score is brought to a concertmaster—he may be a violinist—he is kindly disposed, he looks it over, and casually fastens on a passage "that's bad for the fiddles, it doesn't hang just right, write it like this, they will play it better." But that one phrase is the germ of the whole thing. "Never mind, it will fit the hand better this way—it will sound better." My God! what has sound got to do with music! The waiter brings the only fresh egg he has, but the man at breakfast sends it back because it doesn't fit his eggcup. Why can't music go out in the same way it comes in to a man, without having to crawl over a fence of sounds, thoraxes, catguts, wire, wood, and brass? Consecutive-fifths are as harmless as blue laws compared with the relentless tyranny of the "media." The instrument!—there is the perennial difficulty—there is music's limitations. Why must the scarecrow of the keyboard—the tyrant in terms of the mechanism (be it Caruso or a Jew's-harp) stare into every measure? Is it the composer's fault that man has only ten fingers? Why can't a musical thought be presented as it is born—perchance "a bastard of the slums," or a "daughter of a bishop"—and if it happens to go better later on a bass-drum (than upon a harp) get a good bass-drummer.[1] That music must be heard, is not essential—what it *sounds* like may not be what it *is*. Perhaps the day is coming when music-believers will learn "that silence is a solvent . . . that gives us leave to be universal" rather than personal.

Some fiddler was once honest or brave enough, or perhaps ignorant enough, to say that Beethoven didn't know how to write for the violin,—that, maybe, is one of the many reasons Beethoven is not a Vieuxtemps. Another man says Beethoven's piano sonatas are not pianistic—with a little effort, perhaps, Beethoven could have become a Thalberg. His symphonies are perfect-truths and perfect for the orchestra of 1820—but Mahler could have made them—possibly did make them—we will say, "more perfect," as far as their media clothes are concerned, and Beethoven is to-day big enough to rather like it. He is probably in the same amiable state of mind that the Jesuit priest said, "God was in," when He looked down on the camp ground and saw the priest sleeping with a Congregational Chaplain. Or in the same state of mind you'll be in when you look down and see the sexton keeping your tombstone up to date. The truth of Joachim offsets the repose of Paganini and Kubelik. The repose and reputation of a successful pianist— (whatever that means) who plays Chopin so cleverly that he covers up a sensuality, and in such a way that the purest-minded see nothing but sensuous beauty in it, which, by the way, doesn't disturb him as much as the size of his income-tax—the repose and fame of this man is offset by the truth and obscurity of the village organist who plays Lowell Mason and Bach with such affection that he would give his life rather than lose them. The truth and courage of this organist, who risks his job, to fight the prejudice of the con-gregation, offset the repose and large salary of a more celebrated choirmaster, who holds his job by lowering his ideals, who is willing to let the organ smirk under an insipid, easy-sounding barcarolle for the offertory, who is willing to please the sentimen-tal ears of the music committee (and its wives)—who is more

1 The first movement (Emerson) of the music, which is the cause of all these words, was first thought of (we believe) in terms of a large orches-tra, the second (Hawthorne) in terms of a piano or a dozen pianos, the third (Allcotts)—of an organ (or piano with voice or violin), and the last (Thoreau), in terms of strings, colored possibly with a flute or horn.

willing to observe these forms of politeness than to stand up for a stronger and deeper music of simple devotion, and for a service of a spiritual unity, the kind of thing that Mr. Bossitt, who owns the biggest country place, the biggest bank, and the biggest "House of God" in town (for is it not the divine handiwork of his *own*—pocketbook)—the kind of music that this man, his wife, and *his* party (of property right in pews) can't stand because it isn't "pretty."

The doctrine of this "choice" may be extended to the distinction between literal-enthusiasm and natural-enthusiasm (right or wrong notes, good or bad tones against good or bad interpretation, good or bad sentiment) or between observation and introspection, or to the distinction between remembering and dreaming. Strauss remembers, Beethoven dreams. We see this distinction also in Goethe's confusion of the moral with the intellectual. There is no such confusion in Beethoven—to him they are one. It is told, and the story is so well known that we hesitate to repeat it here, that both these men were standing in the street one day when the Emperor drove by—Goethe, like the rest of the crowd, bowed and uncovered—but Beethoven stood bolt upright, and refused even to salute, saying: "Let him bow to us, for ours is a nobler empire." Goethe's *mind* knew this was true, but his moral courage was not instinctive.

This remembering faculty of "repose," throws the mind in unguarded moments quite naturally towards "manner" and thus to the many things the media can do. It brings on an itching to over-use them—to be original (if anyone will tell what that is) with nothing but numbers to be original with. We are told that a conductor (of the orchestra) has written a symphony requiring an orchestra of one hundred and fifty men. If his work perhaps had one hundred and fifty valuable ideas, the one hundred and fifty men might be justifiable—but as it probably contains not more than a dozen, the composer may be unconsciously ashamed of them, and glad to cover them up under a hundred and fifty men. A man may become famous because he is able to eat nineteen dinners a day, but posterity will decorate his stomach, not his brain.

Manner breeds a cussed-cleverness—only to be clever—a satellite of super-industrialism, and perhaps to be witty in the

bargain, not the wit in mother-wit, but a kind of indoor, artificial, mental arrangement of things quickly put together and
which have been learned and studied—it is of the material and
stays there, while humor is of the emotional and of the approaching spiritual. Even Dukas, and perhaps other Gauls, in their
critical heart of hearts, may admit that "wit" in music, is as impossible as "wit" at a funeral. The wit is evidence of its lack.
Mark Twain could be humorous at the death of his dearest
friend, but in such a way as to put a blessing into the heart of
the bereaved. Humor in music has the same possibilities. But
its quantity has a serious effect on its quality, "inverse ratio" is a
good formula to adopt here. Comedy has its part, but wit never.
Strauss is at his best in these lower rooms, but his comedy reminds us more of the physical fun of Lever rather than "comedy
in the Meredithian sense" as Mason suggests. Meredith is a little
too deep or too subtle for Strauss—unless it be granted that cyn-
icism is more a part of comedy than a part of refined-insult. Let
us also remember that Mr. Disston, not Mr. Strauss, put the
funny notes in the bassoon. A symphony written only to amuse
and entertain is likely to amuse only the writer—and him not
long after the check is cashed.

"Genius is always ascetic and piety and love," thus Emerson
reinforces "God's offer of this choice" by a transcendental definition. The moment a famous violinist refused "to appear" until
he had received his check,—at that moment, *precisely* (assuming
for argument's sake, that this was the first time that materialism
had the ascendency in this man's soul) at that moment he became but a man of "talent"—incidentally, a small man and a
small violinist, regardless of how perfectly he played, regardless
to what heights of emotion he stirred his audience, regardless of
the sublimity of his artistic and financial success.

d'Annunzio, it is told, becoming somewhat discouraged at
the result of some of his Fiume adventures said: "We are the
only Idealists left." This remark may have been made in a
moment of careless impulse, but if it is taken at its face value,
the moment it was made that moment his idealism started down-
hill. A grasp at monopoly indicates that a sudden shift has taken
place from the heights where genius may be found, to the lower
plains of talent. The mind of a true idealist is great enough to

know that a monopoly of idealism or of wheat is a thing nature does not support.

A newspaper music column prints an incident (so how can we assume that it is not true?) of an American violinist who called on Max Reger, to tell him how much he (the American) appreciated his music. Reger gives him a hopeless look and cries: "What! a musician and not speak German!" At that moment, by the clock, regardless of how great a genius he may have been before that sentence was uttered—at that moment he became but a man of "talent." "For the man of talent affects to call his transgressions of the laws of sense trivial and to count them nothing considered with his devotion to his art." His art never taught him prejudice or to wear only one eye. "His art is less for every deduction from his holiness and less for every defect of common sense." And this common sense has a great deal to do with this distinguishing difference of Emerson's between genius and talent, repose and truth, and between all evidences of substance and manner in art. Manner breeds partialists. "Is America a musical nation?"—if the man who is ever asking this question would sit down and think something over he might find less interest in asking it—he might possibly remember that all nations are more musical than any nation, especially the nation that pays the most—and pays the most eagerly, for anything, after it has been professionally—rubber stamped. Music may be yet unborn. Perhaps no music has ever been written or heard. Perhaps the birth of art will take place at the moment, in which the last man, who is willing to make a living out of art is gone and gone forever. In the history of this youthful world the best product that human-beings can boast of is probably, Beethoven—but, maybe, even his art is as nothing in comparison with the future product of some coal-miner's soul in the forty-first century. And the same man who is ever asking about the most musical nation, is ever discovering the most musical man of the most musical nation. When particularly hysterical he shouts, "I have found him! Smith Grabholz—the one great American poet,—at last, here is the Moses the country has been waiting for"—(of course we all know that the country has not been waiting for anybody—and we have many Moses always with us). But the discoverer keeps right on shouting "Here is the one true American poetry, I pro-

nounce it the work of a genius. I predict for him the most brilliant career—for *his* is an art that . . .—for *his* is a soul that . . .
for *his* is a . . ." and Grabholz is ruined;—but ruined, not alone,
by this perennial discoverer of pearls in any oyster-shell
that treats him the best, but ruined by his own (Grabholz's)
talent,—for genius will never let itself be discovered by "a man."
Then the world may ask "Can the one true national "this" or
"that" be killed by its own discoverer?" "No," the country replies, "but each discovery is proof of another impossibility." It is
a sad fact that the one true man and the one true art will never
behave as they should except in the mind of the partialist whom
God has forgotten. But this matters little to him (the man)—his
business is good—for it is easy to sell the future in terms of the
past—and there are always some who will buy anything. The
individual usually *"gains"* if he is willing to but lean on "manner." The evidence of this is quite widespread, for if the discoverer happens to be in any other line of business his sudden
discoveries would be just as important—*to him.* In fact, the theory
of substance and manner in art and its related dualisms, "repose
and truth, genius and talent," &c., may find illustration in many,
perhaps most, of the human activities. And when examined it
(the illustration) is quite likely to show how "manner" is always
discovering partisans. For example, enthusiastic discoveries of the
"paragon" are common in politics—an art to some. These revelations, in this profession are made easy by the pre-election dis-
covering-leaders of the people. And the genius who is discovered,
forthwith starts his speeches of "talent"—though they are hardly
that—they are hardly more than a string of subplatitudes, square-
looking, well-rigged things that almost everybody has seen,
known, and heard since Rome or man fell. Nevertheless these
signs of perfect manner, these series of noble sentiments that the
"noble" never get off, are forcibly, clearly, and persuasively
handed out—eloquently, even beautifully expressed, and with
such personal charm, magnetism, and strength, that their profound messages speed right through the minds and hearts, without as much as spattering the walls, and land right square in
the middle of the listener's vanity. For all this is a part of
manner and its quality is of splendor—for manner is at times a
good bluff but substance a poor one and knows it. The dis-

covered one's usual and first great outburst is probably the greatest truth that he ever utters. Fearlessly standing, he looks straight into the eyes of the populace and with a strong ringing voice (for strong voices and strong statesmanship are inseparable) and with words far more eloquent than the following, he sings "This honor is greater than I deserve but duty calls me—(what, not stated) . . . If elected, I shall be your servant" . . . (for, it is told, that he believes in modesty,—that he has even boasted that he is the most modest man in the country) . . . Thus he has the right to shout, "First, last and forever I am for the people. I am against all bosses. I have no sympathy for politicians. I am for strict economy, liberal improvements and justice! I am also for the—ten commandments" (his intuitive political sagacity keeps him from mentioning any particular one).—But a sublime height is always reached in his perorations. Here we learn that he believes in *honesty*— (repeat *"honesty"*);—we are even allowed to infer that he is one of the very few who know that there is such a thing; and we also learn that since he was a little boy (barefoot) his motto has been "Do Right,"—he swerves not from the right!—he believes in nothing but the right; (to him—everything is right!—if it gets him elected); but cheers invariably stop this great final truth (in brackets) from rising to animate expression. Now all of these translucent axioms are true (are not axioms always true?),—as far as manner is concerned. In other words, the manner functions perfectly. But where is the divine-substance? This is not there—why should it be—if it were *he* might not be there. "Substance" is not featured in this discovery. For the truth of substance is sometimes silence, sometimes ellipses,—and the latter if supplied might turn some of the declarations above into perfect truths,—for instance "first and last and forever I am for the people ('s votes). I'm against all bosses (against me). I have no sympathy for (rival) politicians," etc., etc. But these tedious attempts at comedy should stop,—they're too serious,—besides the illustration may be a little hard on a few, the minority (the non-people) though not on the many, the majority (the people)! But even an assumed parody may help to show what a power manner is for reaction unless it is counter-balanced and then saturated by the other part of the duality. Thus it appears that all there is to this great discovery is that one good politician has discovered another good politician. For manner has brought forth its usual talent;—for manner cannot discover the genius who has discarded platitudes—the genius who has devised a new and surpassing order for mankind, simple and intricate enough, abstract and definite enough, locally impractical and universally practical enough, to wipe out the need for further discoveries of "talent" and incidentally the discoverer's own fortune and political "manner." Furthermore, he (this genius) never will be discovered until the majority-spirit, the common-heart, the human-oversoul, the source of all great values, converts all talent into genius, all manner into substance —until the direct expression of the mind and soul of the majority, the divine right of all consciousness, social, moral, and spiritual, discloses the one true art and thus finally discovers the one true leader—even *itself:*—then no leaders, no politicians, no manner, will hold sway—and no more speeches will be heard.

The intensity to-day, with which techniques and media are organized and used, tends to throw the mind away from a "common sense" and towards "manner" and thus to resultant weak and mental states—for example, the Byronic fallacy—that one who is full of turbid feeling *about himself* is qualified to be some sort of an artist. In this relation "manner" also leads some to think that emotional sympathy for self is as true a part of art as sympathy for others; and a prejudice in favor of the good and bad of one personality against the virtue of many personalities. It may be that when a poet or a whistler becomes conscious that he is in the easy path of any particular idiom,—that he is helplessly prejudiced in favor of any particular means of expression, —that his manner can be catalogued as modern or classic,—that he favors a contrapuntal groove, a sound-coloring one, a sensuous one, a successful one, or a melodious one (whatever that means),—that his interests lie in the French school or the German school, or the school of Saturn,—that he is involved in this particular "that" or that particular "this," or in any particular brand of emotional complexes,—in a word, when he becomes conscious that his style is "his personal own,"—that it has monopolized a geographical part of the world's sensibilities, then it may be that the value of his substance is not growing,—that it even may have started on its way backwards,—it may be that he is trading an inspiration for a bad habit and finally that he is reaching fame, permanence, or some other under-value, and that he is getting farther and farther from a perfect truth. But, on the contrary side of the picture, it is not unreasonable to imagine that if he (this poet, composer, and laborer) is open to all the over-values within his reach,—if he stands unprotected from all the showers of the absolute which may beat upon him,—if he is willing to use or learn to use, or at least if he is not afraid of trying to use, whatever he can, of any and all lessons of the infinite that humanity has received and thrown to man,—that nature has exposed and sacrificed, that life and death have translated—if he accepts all and sympathizes with all, is influenced by all, whether consciously or sub-consciously, drastically or humbly, audibly or inaudibly, whether it be all the virtue of Satan or the only evil of Heaven—and all, even, at one time, even in one chord,—*then* it may be that the value of his substance, and its value to himself, to his art, to all art, even to the Common Soul is growing and approaching nearer and nearer to perfect truths—whatever they are and wherever they may be.

Again, a certain kind of manner-over-influence may be caused by a group-disease germ. The over-influence by, the over-admiration of, and the over-association with a particular artistic personality or a particular type or group of personalities tends to produce equally favorable and unfavorable symptoms, but the unfavorable ones seem to be more contagious. Perhaps the impulse remark of some famous man (whose name we forget) that he "loved music but hated musicians," might be followed (with some good results) at least part of the time. To see the sun rise, a man has but to get up early, and he can always have Bach in his pocket. We hear that Mr. Smith or Mr. Morgan, etc., *et al.* design to establish a "course at Rome," to raise the standard of American music, (or the standard of American composers —which is it?) but possibly the more our composer accepts from his patrons "*et al.*" the less he will accept *from himself*. It may be possible that a day in a "Kansas wheat field" will do more for him than three years in Rome. It may be, that many men—perhaps some of genius— (if you won't admit that all are geniuses) have been started on the downward path of subsidy by trying to write a thousand dollar prize poem or a ten thousand dollar prize opera. How many masterpieces have been prevented from blossoming in this way? A cocktail will make a man eat more, but will not give him a healthy, normal appetite (if he had not that already). If a bishop should offer a "prize living" to the curate who will love God the hardest for fifteen days, whoever gets the prize would love God the least. Such stimulants, it strikes us, tend to industrialize art, rather than develop a spiritual sturdiness —a sturdiness which Mr. Sedgwick says[1] "shows itself in a close union between spiritual life and the ordinary business of life," against spiritual feebleness which "shows itself in the separation of the two." If one's spiritual sturdiness is congenital and somewhat perfect he is not only conscious that this separation has no part in his own soul, but he does not feel its existence in others. He does not believe there is such a thing. But perfection in this respect is rare. And for the most of us, we believe, this sturdiness would be encouraged by anything that will keep or help us keep a normal balance between the spiritual life and the ordinary life. If for every thousand dollar prize a potato field be substituted, so that these candidates of "Clio" can dig a little in real life, perhaps dig up a natural inspiration, arts-air might be a little clearer—a little freer from certain traditional delusions, for instance, that free thought and free love always go to the same café—that atmosphere and diligence are synonymous. To quote Thoreau incorrectly: "When half-Gods talk, the Gods walk!" Everyone should have the opportunity of not being over-influenced.

Again, this over-influence by and over-insistence upon "manner" may finally lead some to believe "that manner for manner's sake is a basis of music." Someone is quoted as saying that "ragtime is the true American music." Anyone will admit that it is one of the many true, natural, and, nowadays, conventional means of expression. It is an idiom, perhaps a "set or series of colloquialisms," similar to those that have added through centuries and through natural means, some beauty to all languages. Every language is but the evolution of slang, and possibly the broad "A" in Harvard may have come down from the "butcher of Southwark." To examine ragtime rhythms and the syncopations of Schumann or of Brahms seems to the writer to show how

[1] H. D. Sedgwick. *The New American Type.* Riverside Press.

much alike they are not. Ragtime, as we hear it, is, of course, more (but not much more) than a natural dogma of shifted accents, or a mixture of shifted and minus accents. It is something like wearing a derby hat on the back of the head, a shuffling lilt of a happy soul just let out of a Baptist Church in old Alabama. Ragtime has its possibilities. But it does not "represent the American nation" any more than some fine old senators represent it. Perhaps we know it now as an ore before it has been refined into a product. It may be one of nature's ways of giving art raw material. Time will throw its vices away and weld its virtues into the fabric of our music. It has its uses as the cruet on the boarding-house table has, but to make a meal of tomato ketchup and horse-radish, to plant a whole farm with sunflowers, even to put a sunflower into every bouquet, would be calling nature something worse than a politician. Mr. Daniel Gregory Mason, whose wholesome influence, by the way, is doing as much perhaps for music in America as American music is, amusingly says: "If indeed the land of Lincoln and Emerson has degenerated until nothing remains of it but a 'jerk and rattle,' then we, at least, are free to repudiate this false patriotism of 'my Country right or wrong,' to insist that better than bad music is no music, and to let our beloved art subside finally under the clangor of the subway gongs and automobile horns, dead, but not dishonored." And so may we ask: Is it better to sing inadequately of the "leaf on Walden floating," and die "dead but not dishonored," or to sing adequately of the "cherry on the cocktail," and live forever?

6

If anyone has been strong enough to escape these rocks—this "Scylla and Charybdis,"—has survived these wrong choices, these under-values with their prizes, Bohemias and heroes, is not such a one in a better position, is he not abler and freer to "declare himself and so to love his cause so singly that he will cleave to it, and forsake all else? What is this cause for the American composer but the utmost musical beauty that he, as an individual man, with his own qualities and defects, is capable of understanding and striving towards?—forsaking all else except those types of musical beauty that come home to him,"[1] and that his spiritual conscience intuitively approves.

"It matters not one jot, provided this course of personal loyalty to a cause be steadfastly pursued, what the special characteristics of the style of the music may be to which one gives one's devotion."[1] This, if over-translated, may be made to mean, what we have been trying to say—that if your interest, enthusiasm, and devotion on the side of substance and truth, are of the stuff to make you so sincere that you sweat—to hell with manner and repose! Mr. Mason is responsible for too many young minds, in their planting season to talk like this, to be as rough, or to go as far, but he would probably admit that, broadly speaking—some such way, *i. e.,* constantly recognizing this ideal duality in art, though not the most profitable road for art to travel, is almost its only way out to eventual freedom and salvation. Sidney Lanier, in a letter to Bayard Taylor writes: "I have so many fair dreams and hopes about music in these days (1875). It is gospel whereof the people are in great need. As Christ gathered up the Ten Commandments and redistilled them into the clear liquid of the wondrous eleventh—love God utterly and thy neighbor as thyself—so I think the time will come when music *rightly developed* to its now little forseen *grandeur* will be found to be a late revelation of all gospels in one." Could the art of music, or the art of anything have a more profound reason for being than this? A conception unlimited by the narrow names of Christian, Pagan, Jew, or Angel! A vision higher and deeper than art itself!

7

The humblest composer will not find true humility in aiming low—he must never be timid or afraid of trying to express that which he feels is far above his power to express, any more than he should be afraid of breaking away, when necessary, from easy first sounds, or afraid of admitting that those half truths that come to him at rare intervals, are half true, for instance, that all art galleries contain masterpieces, which are nothing

1 *Contemporary Composers,* D. G. Mason, Macmillan Co., N. Y.

more than a history of art's beautiful mistakes. He should never fear of being called a high-brow—but not the kind in Prof. Brander Matthews' definition. John L. Sullivan was a "high-brow" in his art. A high-brow can always whip a low-brow.

If he "truly seeks," he "will surely find" many things to sustain him. He can go to a part of Alcott's philosophy—"that all occupations of man's body and soul in their diversity come from but one mind and soul!" If he feels that to subscribe to all of the foregoing and then submit, though not as evidence, the work of his own hands is presumptuous, let him remember that a man is not always responsible for the wart on his face, or a girl for the bloom on her cheek, and as they walk out of a Sunday for an airing, people will see them—but they must have the air. He can remember with Plotinus, "that in every human soul there is the ray of the celestial beauty," and therefore every human outburst may contain a partial ray. And he can believe that it is better to go to the plate and strike out than to hold the bench down, for by facing the pitcher, he may then know the umpire better, and possibly see a new parabola. His presumption, if it be that, may be but a kind of courage Juvenal sings about, and no harm can then be done either side. *"Cantabit vacuus coram latrone viator."*

8

To divide by an arbitrary line something that cannot be divided is a process that is disturbing to some. Perhaps our deductions are not as inevitable as they are logical, which suggests that they are not "logic." An arbitrary assumption is never fair to all any of the time, or to anyone all the time. Many will resent the abrupt separation that a theory of duality in music suggests and say that these general subdivisions are too closely inter-related to be labeled decisively—"this or that." There is justice in this criticism, but our answer is that it is better to be short on the long than long on the short. In such an abstruse art as music it is easy for one to point to this as substance and to that as manner. Some will hold and it is undeniable—in fact quite obvious—that manner has a great deal to do with the beauty of substance, and that to make a too arbitrary division, or distinction between them, is to interfere, to some extent, with an art's beauty and unity. There is a great deal of truth in this too. But on the other hand, beauty in music is too often confused with something that lets the ears lie back in an easy chair. Many sounds that we are used to, do not bother us, and for that reason, we are inclined to call them beautiful. Frequently,—possibly almost invariably,—analytical and impersonal tests will show, we believe, that when a new or unfamiliar work is accepted as beautiful on its first hearing, its fundamental quality is one that tends to put the mind to sleep. A narcotic is not always unnecessary, but it is seldom a basis of progress,—that is, wholesome evolution in any creative experience. This kind of progress has a great deal to do with beauty—at least in its deeper emotional interests, if not in its moral values. (The above is only a personal impression, but it is based on carefully remembered instances, during a period of about fifteen or twenty years.) Possibly the fondness for individual utterance may throw out a skin-deep arrangement, which is readily accepted as beautiful—formulæ that weaken rather than toughen up the musical-muscles. If the composer's sincere conception of his art and of its functions and ideals, coincide to such an extent with these groove-colored permutations of tried out progressions in expediency, that he can arrange them over and over again to his transcendent delight—has he or has he not been drugged with an overdose of habit-forming sounds? And as a result do not the muscles of his clientele become flabbier and flabbier until they give way altogether and find refuge only in a seasoned opera box—where they can *see* without thinking? And unity is too generally conceived of, or too easily accepted as analogous to form, and form (as analogous) to custom, and custom to habit, and habit may be one of the parents of custom and form, and there are all kinds of parents. Perhaps all unity in art, at its inception, is half-natural and half-artificial but time insists, or at least makes us, or inclines to make us feel that it is all natural. It is easy for us to accept it as such. The "unity of dress" for a man at a ball requires a collar, yet he could dance better without it. Coherence, to a certain extent, must bear some relation to the listener's subconscious perspective. For example, a critic has to listen to a thousand concerts a year, in which there is much repetition, not only of the same pieces, but the same formal relations of tones, cadences, progressions, etc. There is present a certain routine series of image-necessity-stimulants, which he doesn't seem to need until they disappear. Instead of listening to music, he listens around it. And from this subconscious viewpoint, he inclines perhaps more to the thinking about than thinking in music. If he could go into some other line of business for a year or so perhaps his perspective would be more naturally normal. The unity of a sonata movement has long been associated with its form, and to a greater extent than is necessary. A first theme, a development, a second in a related key and its development, the free fantasia, the recapitulation, and so on, and over again. Mr. Richter or Mr. Parker may tell us that all this is natural, for it is based on the classic-song form, but in spite of your teachers a vague feeling sometimes creeps over you that the form-nature of the song has been stretched out into deformity. Some claim for Tchaikowsky that his clarity and coherence of design is unparalleled (or some such word) in works for the orchestra. That depends, it seems to us, on how far repetition is an essential part of clarity and coherence. We know that butter comes from cream—but how long must we watch the "churning arm!" If nature is not enthusiastic about explanation, why should Tschaikowsky be? Beethoven had to churn, to some extent, to make his message carry. He had to pull the ear, hard and in the same place and several times, for the 1790 ear was tougher than the 1890 one. But the "great Russian weeper" might have spared us. To Emerson, "unity and the over-soul, or the common-heart, are synonymous." Unity is at least nearer to these than to solid geometry, though geometry may be all unity.

But to whatever unpleasantness the holding to this theory of duality brings us, we feel that there is a natural law underneath it all, and like all laws of nature, a liberal interpretation is the one nearest the truth. What part of these supplements are opposites? What part of substance is manner? What part of this duality is polarity? These questions though not immaterial may be disregarded, if there be a sincere appreciation (intuition is always sincere) of the "divine" spirit of the thing. Enthusiasm for, and recognition of these higher over these lower values will transform a destructive iconoclasm into creation, and a mere devotion into consecration—a consecration which, like Amphion's music, will raise the Walls of Thebes.

9

Assuming, and then granting, that art-activity can be transformed or led towards an eventual consecration, by recognizing and using in their true relation, as much as one can, these higher and lower dual values—and that the doing so is a part, if not the whole of our old problem of paralleling or approving in art the highest attributes, moral and spiritual, one sees in life—if you will grant all this, let us offer a practical suggestion—a thing that one who has imposed the foregoing should try to do just out of common decency, though it be but an attempt, perhaps, to make his speculations less speculative, and to beat off metaphysics.

All, men-bards with a divine spark, and bards without, feel the need at times of an inspiration from without, "the breath of another soul to stir our inner flame," especially when we are in pursuit of a part of that "utmost musical beauty," that we are capable of understanding—when we are breathlessly running to catch a glimpse of that unforeseen grandeur of Mr. Lanier's dream. In this beauty and grandeur perhaps marionettes and their souls have a part—though how great their part is, we hear, is still undetermined; but it is morally certain that, at times, a part with itself must be some of those greater contemplations that have been caught in the "World's Soul," as it were, and nourished for us there in the soil of its literature.

If an interest in, and a sympathy for, the thought-visions of men like Charles Kingsley, Marcus Aurelius, Whittier, Montaigne, Paul of Tarsus, Robert Browning, Pythagoras, Channing, Milton, Sophocles, Swedenborg, Thoreau, Francis of Assisi, Wordsworth, Voltaire, Garrison, Plutarch, Ruskin, Ariosto, and all kindred spirits and souls of great measure, from David down to Rupert Brooke,—if a study of the thought of such men creates a sympathy, even a love for them and their ideal-part, it is certain that this, however inadequately expressed, is nearer to what music was given man for, than a devotion to "Tristan's sensual love of Isolde," to the "Tragic Murder of a Drunken Duke," or to the sad thoughts of a bathtub when the water is being let out. It matters little here whether a man who paints a picture of a useless beautiful landscape *imperfectly* is a greater genius than the man who paints a useful bad smell *perfectly*.

It is not intended in this suggestion that inspirations coming from the higher planes should be limited to any particular thought or work, as the mind receives it. The plan rather embraces all that should go with an expression of the composite-value. It is of the underlying spirit, the direct unrestricted imprint of one soul on another, a portrait, not a photograph of the personality—it is the ideal part that would be caught in this canvas. It is a sympathy for "substance"—the over-value together with a consciousness that there must be a lower value—the "Demosthenic part of the Philippics"—the "Ciceronic part of the Catiline," the sublimity, against the vileness of Rousseau's *Confessions*. It is something akin to, but something more than these predominant partial tones of Hawthorne—"the grand old countenance of Homer; the decrepit form, but vivid face of Æsop; the dark presence of Dante; the wild Ariosto; Rabelais' smile of deep-wrought mirth; the profound, pathetic humor of Cervantes; the all-glorious Shakespeare; Spenser, meet guest for allegoric structure; the severe divinity of Milton; and Bunyan, molded of humblest clay, but instinct with celestial fire."

There are communities now, partly vanished, but cherished and sacred, scattered throughout this world of ours, in which freedom of thought and soul, and even of body, have been fought for. And we believe that there ever lives in that part of the over-soul, native to them, the thoughts which these freedom-struggles have inspired. America is not too young to have its divinities, and its place legends. Many of those "Transcendent Thoughts" and "Visions" which had their birth beneath our Concord elms—messages that have brought salvation to many listening souls throughout the world—are still growing, day by day, to greater and greater beauty—are still showing clearer and clearer man's way to God!

No true composer will take his substance from another finite being—but there are times, when he feels that his self-expression needs some liberation from at least a part of his own soul. At such times, shall he not better turn to those greater souls, rather than to the external, the immediate, and the "Garish Day"?

The strains of one man may fall far below the course of those Phaetons of Concord, or of the Ægean Sea, or of Westmorland —but the greater the distance his music falls away, the more reason that some greater man shall bring his nearer those higher spheres.

Index to Monsieur Croche the Dilettante Hater